Camino de Santiago

✝

St. Jean Pied de Port – Santiago de Compostela

maps - mapas - mappe mapy - karten - cartes

John Brierley

4

ISBN: 978-1-84409-714-2

British Library Cataloguing-in-Publication Data.
A catalogue record for this book is available from the British Library.

All photographs © John Brierley 2017
All maps © John Brierley 2017

Traducción española: Lanzada Calatayud Alvarez
Tradução portuguesa: José Luis Sanches
Traduction française: Jean-François Courouau
Deutsch ubersetzung: Hannah Albrecht
Traduzione italiano: Monica Sandra Lista Rodriguez
Nederlandse vertaling: Hans Lankhaar
Tłumaczenie polskie: Emil Mendyk

Printed and bound in the European Union

Published by
CAMINO GUIDES
An imprint of Findhorn Press Ltd
117-121 High Street
Forres IV36 1AB
Scotland

Tel: +44(0)1309-690582
Fax: +44(0)131-777-2711

Email: info@findhornpress.com
www.findhornpress.com
www.caminoguides.com

Download our Mobile Application

Available on iOS, Android and Windows Phone 8

eCamino

www.ecamino.eu

5

33 Stages / Etapas / Stufen / Stadi / Estágios / Étapes / Stadia / Etapy

St Jean Pied de Port – Santiago de Compostela 778.5 km (**483.7** miles)

Map symbols used in this guide:

Total km — Total distance for stage map
     Adjusted for climb (100m vertical = additional 0.5km)
(850m) **Alto ▲** — Contours / High point of each stage
< **Ⓐ Ⓗ** > — Intermediate accommodation
◄ **3.5** — Precise distance between points (3.5 km = ± 1 hour)
→•150m > / ^ / < — Interim distances •150 metres turn right> / straight on^ / <left

.... / .... — Path or track (*green: natural path* / *grey: concrete or senda*)
——○—— — Secondary road (*grey: asphalt*) / Roundabout *rotonda*
—— N-11 —— — Main road [N-] *Nacional* (*red: additional traffic and hazard*)
—— A-1 —— — Motorway *autopista* (*blue: conventional motorway colour*)
+++++++•• — Railway *ferrocarril* / Station *estación*

X ? Ø — Crossing *cruce* / Option *opción* / Extra care *¡cuidado!*
● ● ● ● ● — Main route (*yellow: ± 80% of pilgrims*)
● ● ● ● ● — Alternative road route (*grey: more asphalt*)
● ● ● ● ● — Scenic route (*green: more remote / less waymarks & facilities*)
● ● ● ● ● — Optional detour *desvío* (*turquoise*) to point of interest

🗼 ⚶ 📡 — Windmill / Viewpoint *punto de vista* / Radio mast
▪—·—·/·—·— — National boundary / Provincial boundary *límite provincial*
~ / ~ — River *río* / Stream *arroyo*
◯ / ◯ — Sea or lake *Mar o lago* / Woodland *bosques*
✝ ⊥ ✝ — Church *iglesia* / Chapel *capilla* / Wayside cross *cruceiro*

Ⓖ ☕ Ⓤ — Drinking font *fuente agua potable* / Café / Shop *minimercado*
menú V. — *menú peregrino* 3 course meal + wine / *V. Vegetariano*
ℹ 🏠 ✕ — Tourist office *turismo* / Manor house *casa señorial* / Picnic
➕ ✚ ✉ — Pharmacy *farmacia* / Hospital / Post office *correos*
✈ 🚌 ⛽ — Airport / Bus station *estación de autobús* / gasolinera
⁙ XIIᵗʰc — Ancient monument / 12ᵗʰ century

Ⓐ❶ Ⓙ — Pilgrim hostel(s) *Albergue* / Youth hostel *Juventude*
Ⓗ Ⓟ Ⓒ — Hotels *H-H*****€30-90 / Pension *P**€20+ / B&B *CR* €35+
Ⓗ Ⓐ Ⓙ — (off route accommodation *alojamiento fuera de ruta*)
[32] — Number of bed spaces (usually bunk beds *literas*)
[÷4]+ — ÷ number of rooms / + additional private rooms €20+
Par. — Parish hostel *Parroquial* donation / €5
Conv. — Convent or monastery hostel *donativo* / €5
Muni. — Municipal hostel €5+
Xunta — Galician government *Xunta* hostel €6
Asoc. — Association hostel €7+
Priv. (*) — Private hostel (network*) €10+ / Incl. *including breakfast*
     Prices are approximate; for comparison purposes only
▭ — Town plan *plan de la ciudad* with page number
(Pop.–Alt. m) — Town population and altitude in metres
▭ — City suburbs *suburbios de la ciudad* (*grey*)
▭ — Historical centre *centro histórico* (*brown*)

Introduction: We all have too much paraphernalia in our lives – in an effort to lighten the load we have produced this slim edition of maps. This has been made possible by the selfless work of pilgrim associations that have waymarked the route such that, today, we need only the barest information to get us to our destination. It would be difficult to get lost if we remain present to each moment and attentive for the yellow arrows that point the way to Santiago – mindfulness is the key. Take time to familiarise yourself with the map symbols opposite.

The standard and cost of pilgrim accommodation ranges from parish hostels by donation and municipal hostels offering basic facilities from €5 (no prior booking) to private hostels from €10+ but generally with additional facilities such as washing and drying machines *secadora*. The latter a real boon in wet weather. A basic 3 course main meal with wine *menú peregrino* from €9.

These multilingual maps recognise the international fellowship of the camino. This helps to foster a sense of camaraderie and communion; a shared spiritual intention that lies at the heart of pilgrimage. It is this transcendent focus that distinguishes pilgrimage from long distance walking. We recommend you source a guidebook with notes on how best to prepare for an extended trip of this nature such as the companion book *A Pilgrim's Guide to the Camino Francés a practical & mystical manual for the modern day pilgrim.*

All of us travel two paths simultaneously; the outer path along which we haul our body and the inner pathway of soul. We need to be mindful of both and take time to prepare ourselves accordingly. The traditional way of the pilgrim is to travel alone, by foot, carrying all the material possessions we might need for the journey ahead. This provides the first lesson for the pilgrim – to leave behind all that is superfluous and to travel with only the barest necessities. Preparation for the inner path is similar – we start by letting go of psychic waste accumulated over the years such as resentments, prejudices and outmoded belief systems. With an open mind and open heart we will more readily assimilate the lessons to be found along this ancient Path of Enquiry.

We have been asleep a long time. Despite the chaotic world around us, or perhaps because of it, something is stirring us to awaken from our collective amnesia. A sign of this awakening is the number of people drawn to walk the caminos. The hectic pace of modern life, experienced not only in our work but also our family and social lives, spins us ever outwards away from our centre. We have allowed ourselves to be thrown onto the surface of our lives – mistaking busy-ness for aliveness, but this superficial existence is inherently unsatisfying.

Pilgrimage offers us an opportunity to slow down and allow some spaciousness into our lives. In this quieter space we can reflect on the deeper significance of our lives and the reasons why we came here. The camino encourages us to ask the perennial question – Who am I? And, crucially, it provides time for answers to be understood and integrated. So don't rush the camino – take the time it takes because it may well prove a pivotal turning point in your life.

Whichever route we take, our ultimate Destination is assured. The only choice we have is how long it takes us to arrive *buen camino.*

John Brierley

Claves para las leyendas del mapa:

Total km	Distancia total de la etapa indicada
▲	Adaptado para el desnivel (100 m verticales = a 0,5 km adicionales)
(850m) **Alto ▲**	Curva de desnivel / Punto más elevado de cada etapa
< A H >	Alojamiento intermedio
◄ 3.5	Distancia exacta entre puntos (3,5 km = ± 1 hora de camino)
→150m > / ^ / <	Distancias parciales: a150 m a la derecha> / seguir recto / <a la izquierda
.... /	Camino o sendero (*verde*: caminos naturales / *gris*: hormigón)
══○══	Carretera secundaria (*gris*: asfalto) / Rotonda
▬▬ N-11 ▬▬	Carretera principal [N-] (*rojo*: mayor tráfico y peligro)
══ A-1 ══	Autopista (*azul*: color habitual)
++++++●	Vía de tren / / Estación de ferrocarril
X ? ‖	Cruce / Punto de Opción / Atención especial
● ● ● ● ●	Ruta principal (*amarillo*: ± 80% peregrinos)
● ● ● ● ●	Ruta por carretera (*gris*: más asfalto)
● ● ● ● ●	Ruta escénica (*verde*: más alejada / menos servicios)
● ● ● ● ●	Rodeo opcional a un punto de interés (*turquesa*)
⌂ ☼ 工	Molino de viento / Punto de vista / Antena de radio
·—·/·—·	Frontera estatal / Límites de provinciales
∼ / ∼	Río / Arroyo
◯ / ◯	Lago o estuario / Bosque
♰ ♱ †	Iglesia / Capilla / Crucero
⊕ ☕ ♨	Fuente de agua potable / Café / Mini-mercado
menú *V.*	Menu peregrino ±€9 / *V.* Vegetariano
ℹ ⌂ ✕	Turismo / Casa señorial / Picnic
✚ ✚ ✉	Farmacia / Hospital / Oficina de correos
⊕ 🚏 ⛽	Aeropuerto / Estación de autobús / Gasolinera
∴ XII.ᵗʰc	Monumento histórico / Siglo XII
A❶ J	Albergue(s) de peregrinos / Albergue juvenil
H P C	Hoteles *H–H***** €30–90 / Pensión *P* €20+ / Casa rural *CR €35+*
Ⓗ Ⓐ Ⓙ	Alojamiento *fuera* de ruta
[32]	Número de plazas de cama (normalmente literas)
[÷4]+	÷ número de dormitorios + *también habitaciones privadas €20+*
Par.	Albergue parroquial *donación* / €5
Conv.	Albergue en un convento o monasterio *donación* / €5+
Muni.	Albergue municipal €5+
Xunta	Albergue de la Xunta de Galicia €6
Asoc.	Albergue de una asociación €7+
Priv. (*)	Albergue privado (de la Red de Albergues*) €10 (incl.=+desayuno)
	Todos los precios son aproximados y sólo a efectos comparativos
☐	Plano de ciudad
(Pop.–Alt. m)	Población – Altitud en metros
▭	Periferia (*gris*)
▭	Centro Histórico (*marrón*)

Introducción: En las vidas de todos nosotros hay un exceso de parafernalia. Con la pretensión de aligerar la carga, hemos creado esta delgada edición de mapas. Ello ha sido posible gracias al trabajo desinteresado de las asociaciones de peregrinos que han señalizado el recorrido de tal forma que, hoy en día, tan solo necesitamos la información más básica para alcanzar nuestro destino. Resulta difícil perderse si en todo momento permanecemos concentrados y atentos a las flechas amarillas que apuntan en dirección a Santiago: en la concentración está la clave. Tómate un tiempo para familiarizarte con los símbolos del mapa que hallarás en la página de enfrente.

El estándar y el costo de alojamiento peregrino varía de los albergues municipales que ofrece servicios básicos de € 5 (sin reserva previa) a los albergues privados a partir de € 10 + pero a menudo con servicios adicionales tales como lavadoras y secadoras. Un menú peregrino comprende una comida básica de 3 platos con vino a un costo de alrededor de 9 €.

Estos mapas multilingües son un reconocimiento al compañerismo internacional del camino. Éste favorece el sentimiento de camaradería y comunión; una intención espiritual compartida que yace en el corazón de la peregrinación. Es esta focalización transcendente lo que distingue al peregrinaje del senderismo de larga distancia. Te recomendamos usar una guía con notas sobre cómo preparar bien un viaje largo de esta naturaleza, como el libro complementario *A Pilgrim's Guide to the Camino Francés*, un manual práctico y místico para el peregrino moderno *(Inglés)*.

Todos recorremos dos caminos simultáneamente: el camino exterior, por el que arrastramos nuestro cuerpo, y el camino interior del alma. Debemos ser conscientes de los dos y tomarnos el tiempo para prepararnos adecuadamente. El camino tradicional del peregrino es viajar solo, a pie, cargando con todas las posesiones materiales que podamos necesitar en el viaje que tenemos por delante. Esto brinda la primera lección al peregrino: dejar atrás todo lo supérfluo y viajar tan sólo con lo estrictamente necesario. La preparación para el camino interior es similar: comenzamos soltando la basura psíquica acumulada a lo largo de los años, como resentimientos, prejuicios y sistemas de creencias pasados de moda. Con una mente y un corazón abiertos asimilaremos con mayor facilidad las lecciones con las que nos encontraremos a lo largo de este Camino de las Averiguaciones.

Llevamos mucho tiempo dormidos. Pese al caótico mundo que nos rodea, o tal vez a causa de él, hay algo que nos sacude para que despertemos de nuestra amnesia colectiva. Una señal de este despertar es el número de personas que se sienten atraídas por hacer los caminos. El ritmo frenético de la vida moderna, que experimentamos no sólo en el trabajo sino también en nuestra vida familiar y en la social, hace que cada vez revoloteamos más lejos de nuestro centro. Hemos consentido en ser arrojados a la superficie de nuestras vidas, al confundir estar ocupados con estar vivos, pero esta existencia superficial resulta intrínsecamente insatisfactoria.

La peregrinación nos brinda la oportunidad de reducir el ritmo y de dotar a nuestras vidas de una cierta amplitud. En este espacio más tranquilo se puede reflexionar acerca del significado más profundo de nuestras vidas y las razones por las que hemos venido aquí. El camino nos anima a hacernos la pregunta perenne: ¿quién soy? Y, lo que resulta crucial, nos proporciona el tiempo para poder comprender y asimilar las respuestas. Así que no te apresures en recorrer el camino: tómate el tiempo que sea necesario, porque podría resultar ser el punto de inflexión de tu vida.

Buen camino.

Zeichenerklärung:

Total km	Gesamtentfernung für angezeigte Etappe
▲	An Höhenunterschied angepasst (100 m Höhe = zusätzliche 0,5 km)
(850m) **Alto ▲**	Etappenprofil / Höchster Punkt jeder Etappe
< ⓐ ⓗ >	Unterkunft unterwegs
◀ **3.5**	Genaue Entfernung zwischen Punkten (3,5 km = ± 1 Stunde Wandern)
→150m > / ^ / <	Zwischenentfernungen – in 150 m nach rechts> / geradeaus^ /
	<nach links
.... /	Weg oder Pfad (*grün*: natürliche Wege / *grau*: beton)
═══○═══	Nebenstraße (*grau*: Asphalt) / Kreisverkehr
═══ N-11	Hauptstraße [N-] (*rot*: mehr Verkehr und größere Gefahr)
═══ A-1	Autobahn (*blau*: herkömmliche Farbe)
++++++●	Bahn / Bahnhof
X ? ⓿	Kreuzung / Optionspunkt / Besondere Vorsicht
● ● ● ● ●	Hauptroute (*gelb*: ± 80% pilger / vorwiegend Wege)
● ● ● ● ●	Landstraßen-Route (*grau*: mehr Asphalt)
● ● ● ● ●	Route mit Ausblick (*grün*: abgelegener / weniger Versorgung)
● ● ● ● ●	Möglicher Abstecher *desvío* zu Sehenswürdigkeit (*türkis*)
↑ �▽ ↑	Windrad / Aussichtspunkt / Antennenmast
·▬·/·▬·	Landesgrenze / Provinzgrenze
∼ / ∼	Fluss / Bach
◯ / ◯	See oder Flussmündung / Wald
✝ ⸸ ✝	Kirche / Kapelle / Kreuz am Wegesrand
Ⓖ ☕ ♙	Trinkwasser-Quelle / Café Bar / Mini-Markt
menú V.	Restaurant mit Pilgermenü *menú* / Vegetarisch
ⓩ 🏛 ✗	Tourismus / Herrenhaus / Picknick-Tisch
✚ ✚ ✉	Apotheke / Krankenhaus / Post
⊕ ⊟ �ⵎ	Flughafen / Busbahnhof / Tankstelle
♣ XII[th]c	Altes Denkmal / 12. Jahrhundert
Ⓐ❶ Ⓙ	Pilgerherberge(n) / Jugendherberge
Ⓗ Ⓟ Ⓒ	Hotel *H**–*H***** €30–90 /Pension *P* €20+ / Zimmer Incl.** *CR* €35+
Ⓗ Ⓐ Ⓙ	*Unterkunft abseits der Route*
[32]	Anzahl der Bettplätze (gewöhnlich Etagenbetten)
[÷4]+	÷ Anzahl der Schlafsäle + *auch Privatzimmer* €20+
Par.	Gemeinde-Herberge (Kirchengemeinde) Spende *donación* (€5)
Conv.	Klosterherberge Spende *donación* (€5+)
Muni.	Städtische Herberge €5+
Xunta	Herberge der Landesregierung Galiziens (Xunta) €6
Asoc.	Herberge einer Vereinigung €7+
Priv. (*)	Private Herberge (privates Netzwerk*) €10+ / Incl.** mit Frühstück
	Alle Preise sind annähernd und nur zum Vergleich angegeben
▢	Stadtplan
(Pop.–Alt. m)	Außenbezirke (*grau*)
	Altstadt *centro histórico* (*braun*)
▢	Stadtbevölkerung – Höhe in Metern

Einführung: Wir alle haben zu viel Trödel in unserem Leben – um die Last zu erleichtern, haben wir diese schlanke Karten-Edition hergestellt. Ermöglicht wurde dies durch die selbstlose Arbeit von Pilgerorganisationen, die die Route dergestalt markiert haben, dass wir heute nur die grundlegendste Information brauchen, um an unser Ziel zu gelangen. Es ist schwer, sich zu verlaufen; wir müssen nur in jedem Moment gegenwärtig sein und auf die gelben Pfeile achten, die den Weg nach Santiago weisen – Achtsamkeit ist der Schlüssel. Nimm dir Zeit, dich mit den Karten-Symbolen auf der gegenüberliegenden Seite vertraut zu machen.

Der Standard und die Kosten der Pilger Unterkunft variiert von *Xunta* Hostels bieten grundlegende Einrichtungen ab € 5 (kein Vorreservierung) an private Hostels ab € 10 +, aber oft mit zusätzlichen Einrichtungen wie Waschmaschinen und Trockner. Eine grundlegende 3-Gänge-Menü mit Wein *(menú peregrino)* kostet ca. € 9.

Die mehrsprachigen Karten würdigen die internationale Gemeinschaft des Camino. Dieser för¬dert das Gefühl von Freundschaft und Vereinigung; ein ge¬meinsames geistiges Ansinnen, das im Herzen der Wallfahrt liegt. Es ist dieser Fokus auf das Transzendente, was eine Wallfahrt vom Fernwandern unter¬scheidet.

Wir alle reisen gleichzeitig auf zwei Wegen; der äußere, entlang dessen wir unseren Körper schleppen, und der innere Weg der Seele. Wir müssen uns beider bewusst sein und uns die Zeit nehmen für eine entsprechende Vorbereitung. Traditionsgemäß ist der Weg des Wallfahrers eine Reise zu Fuß, alleine; wir tragen allen materiellen Besitz, den wir für die bevorstehende Fahrt benötigen mögen, mit uns. Dies bringt auch die erste Lektion für den Pilger – alles Überflüssige hinter sich zu lassen und nur mit dem wahrhaft Notwendigen zu reisen. Die Vorbereitung für den inneren Weg ist ähnlich – sie beginnt mit dem Ablegen vom psychischen Müll, der sich über die Jahre angehäuft hat, wie Groll, Vorurteile und überholte Glaubenssysteme. Mit offenem Verstand und offenem Herzen werden wir umso leichter die Lehren aufnehmen, die entlang dieses uralten Weges der Suche gefunden werden können.

Wir haben lange geschlafen. Trotz der chaotischen Welt um uns herum, oder vielleicht gerade ihretwegen, schüttelt uns etwas, auf dass wir aus unserer kollektiven Amnesie erwachen. Ein Zeichen dieses Erwachens ist die Anzahl der Menschen, die sich angezogen fühlen, die Caminos zu erwandern. Das hektische Tempo des modernen Lebens, das wir nicht nur in unserer Arbeit, sondern auch in unserem familiären und gesellschaftlichen Leben erfahren, wirbelt uns immer weiter nach außen, weg von unserem Zentrum. Wir haben es zugelassen, an die Oberfläche unseres Lebens geworfen zu werden – wir verwechseln Geschäftigkeit mit Lebendigkeit, doch dieses oberflächliche Dasein ist in sich unbefriedigend.

Eine Wallfahrt bietet uns die Gelegenheit, langsamer zu werden und etwas Weite in unser Leben hineinzulassen. In diesem stilleren Umfeld können wir über die tiefere Bedeutung unseres Lebens nachdenken und über den Grund, wozu wir hierher kamen. Der Camino ermutigt uns, die immerwährende Frage zu stellen – wer bin ich? Und entscheidend ist: er bietet uns Zeit dafür, die Antworten zu verstehen und zu integrieren. Also hetzt nicht auf dem Camino – nimm dir die Zeit, die er erfordert, denn er könnte sich als ein entscheidender Wendepunkt in deinem Leben entpuppen.

Buen camino.

Legenda:

Total km — Distanza totale della tappa

Adattato al dislivello (100 m verticali = a 0,5 km addizionali)

(850m) **Alto ▲** — Curva di dislivello / Punto più elevato di ogni tappa

< 🅐 🄷 > — Alloggio intermedio

◀ 3.5 — Distanza esatta tra punti (3,5 km = ± 1 ora di cammino)

–● 150m > / ^ / < — Distanze parziali: a 150 m a destra > / proseguire dritto ^ / < a sinistra

⬛⬛⬛⬛⬛ / ⬜⬜⬜⬜⬜ — Cammino o sentiero (*verde*:cammini naturali /*grigio*:calcestruzzo)

═══○═══ — Strada secondaria (*grigio*: asfalto) / Rotonda

═══N-11═══ — Strada principale [N-] (*rosso*: maggiore traffico e pericolo)

═══A-1═══ — Autostrada (*azzurra*: colore abituale)

+++++++● — Ferrovia / Stazione

🅇 ⁉ ❗ — Croce / Punto di Opzione / Particolare attenzione!

● ● ● ● ● — Itinerario principale (*giallo*: ± 80% dei pellegrini)

● ● ● ● ● — Itinerario per strada (*grigio*: più asfalto)

● ● ● ● ● — Itinerario panoramico (*verde*: più remoto / meno servizi)

● ● ● ● ● — Deviazione opzionale a un punto di interesse (*azzurrino*)

↑ ☼ 🎙 — Mulino a vento / Belvedere / Antenna radio

▬▬ · / · ▬▬ — Frontiera statale / Limiti provinciali

∼ / ∼ — Fiume / Ruscello

◯ / ◯ — Lago oppure estuario / Bosco

‡ ⸸ † — Chiesa / Cappella / Calvario

🅕 ☕ 🏪 — Fontana di acqua potabile / Caffè bar / Mini-mercato

menú V. — Ristorante *menú del peregrino* / Vegetariano

🄸 🏨 ✕ — Turismo / Casa signorile / Picnic

✚ ⊕ ✉ — Farmacia / Ospedale / Posta

✈ 🚌 ⛽ — Aeroporto / Stazione degli autobus / Distributore di benzina

⁛ XIIth c — Monumento storico / Secolo XII

🄰① 🄹 — Ostello (-i) del pellegrino *Alb.* / Ostello della la gioventù

🄷 🄿 🄲 — Hotel *H°–H°°°°* 30–90 / Pensione *P* €20+ / Casa Rurale Incl.*CR* €35+

Ⓗ Ⓐ Ⓙ — *Alloggio fuori itinerario*

[32] — Numero di posti letto (in genere letti a castello)

[÷4]+ — ÷ numero di stanze / + *anche stanze private* €20+

Par. — Ostello parrocchiale *donazione (€5+)*

Conv. — Ostello in un convento o monastero *donazione (€5+)*

Muni. — Ostello municipale €5+

Xunta — Ostello della Xunta di Galizia €6

Asoc. — Ostello di un'associazione €7

Priv. (*) — Ostello privato (Rete di Ostelli*) €10+ / Incl. Compresa la colazione
I prezzi sono indicativi; ai soli fini comparativi

⬜ — Cartina della città

(Pop.–Alt. m) — Popolazione – Altitudine in metri

⬜ — Periferia (*grigio*)

⬛ — Centro Storico (*marrone*)

Introduzione: Nelle vite di tutti noi c'è un eccesso di accessori. Per cercare di alleggerire il carico, abbiamo creato questa edizione di mappe ,leggera'. Questo è stato possibile grazie al lavoro disinteressato delle Associazioni di Pellegrini che hanno segnato il percorso, il che fa sì che oggi ci bastino poche informazioni di base per raggiungere la destinazione. È difficile perdersi se si rimane costantemente concentrati e attenti alle frecce gialle che puntano verso Santiago: la chiave è l'attenzione. Prendi il tempo necessario per familiarizzarti con i simboli della mappa che trovi nella pagina di fronte.

Il comfort e il costo degli alloggi per i pellegrini varia dagli ostelli parrocchiali, che chiedono una libera offerta, a quelli municipali, che offrono servizi di base a partire da €5 (senza obbligo di prenotazione), agli ostelli privati che vanno dai €10 in su, ma che spesso offrono servizi aggiuntivi come lavatrice e asciugatrice, quest'ultima una gran comodità nei giorni di pioggia. Un pasto base di 3 portate con vino (menú peregrino) costa circa €9.

Queste cartine multilingue sono un riconoscimento alla fratellanza internazionale del Cammino. Questa favorisce il sentimento di cameratismo e comunione: un'intenzione spirituale condivisa che costituisce il cuore del pellegrinaggio. È questo che distingue il pellegrinaggio dal trekking di lunga distanza.

Tutti percorriamo simultaneamente due cammini: il cammino esteriore, che percorriamo fisicamente, e quello interiore dell'anima. Dobbiamo affrontare tutti e due con consapevolezza, e prenderci il tempo necessario per preparaci adeguatamente. Tradizionalmente il pellegrino viaggia da solo, a piedi, portandosi dietro tutto ciò di cui ha bisogno per il viaggio. In questo modo il pellegrino impara la prima lezione: lasciare indietro tutto il superfluo e viaggiare solo con quanto strettamente necessario. La preparazione per il cammino interiore è simile: si comincia buttando via la spazzatura psichica accumulata lungo gli anni, come risentimenti, pregiudizi e sistemi di credenze obsoleti. Con una mente e un cuore aperti si assimilano più facilmente le lezioni che si imparano lungo questo antico Cammino di Ricerca.

È da tanto tempo che siamo addormentati. Malgrado il mondo caotico che ci gira attorno, o forse proprio grazie ad esso, sentiamo qualcosa che ci spinge a svegliarci dalla nostra amnesia collettiva. Un segnale di questo risveglio è il numero di persone che si sentono attratte dai pellegrinaggi. Il ritmo frenetico della vita moderna, non solo al lavorativa ma anche famigliare e sociale, ci spinge sempre più lontano dal nostro centro. Ci lasciamo trascinare sempre più verso aspetti superficiali delle nostre vite, confondendo l'essere occupati con l'essere vivi, ma questa esistenza superficiale risulta sostanzialmente insoddisfacente.

Il pellegrinaggio ci offre l'occasione di rallentare il ritmo e di dare un po' di respiro alla nostra vita. In questo spazio più tranquillo possiamo riflettere sul significato profondo della vita e sulle ragioni per cui siamo venuti qui. Il Cammino ci spinge a farci l'eterna domanda: chi sono io? E, cosa più importante, ci da il tempo di poter capire e assimilare le risposte. Quindi non percorrere il Cammino di fretta: prendi il tempo di cui hai bisogno, perché potrebbe diventare un punto di svolta della tua vita.

Buen camino.

Légende:

Total km — Distance totale de l'étape

Distance équivalente avec ajout de la déclivité (100 m vertical =

*(850m)***Alto**▲ — Courbes de niveau / Point culminant de l'étape / 0,5 km add.)

< 🅐 🅗 > — Hébergement en cours d'étape

◀ **3.5** — Distance précise entre points (3,5 km = ± 1 heure de marche)

─●150m > / ^ / < — Distances intermédiaires : à 150m tourner à droite> / ^tout droit / à gauche>

.... / .... — Sentier ou piste (*vert* : en terre / *gris*: béton)

══●══ — Route secondaire (*gris*: asphalte) / Rond-point

══ **N-11** ══ — Route principale [N]-(*rouge* : circulation plus importante et danger)

══ **A-1** ══ — Autoroute (*bleu*: couleur conventionnelle)

++++++● — Voie ferrée / Gare

X **?** **❶** — Carrefour / Point de l'option / Faire particulièrement attention

● ● ● ● ● — Route principale (*jaune*: ± 80% des pèlerins)

● ● ● ● ● — Itinéraire par la route (*gris* : plus d'asphalte)

● ● ● ● ● — Route panoramique (*vert*: moins de services / plus à l'écart)

● ● ● ● ● — Détour facultatif vers un point d'intérêt (*turquoise*)

↑ ☇ ↑ — Moulin à vent / Point de vue / Antenne radio

·—·/·—·— — Frontière nationale / limite de province

～/～ — Rivière / Ruisseau

◯/◯ — Lac ou estuaire / Forêt

✝ ♦ ✝ — Église / Chapelle / Croix

🅖 ➤ 🅦 — Fontaine d'eau potable / Café-bar / Supérette

menú *V.* — restaurant avec menu du pèlerin / Végétarien

🄱 🏠 ✕ — Tourisme / Quinta ou manoir / table de pique-nique

➕ ➕ ✉ — Pharmacie / Hôpital / Poste

⊕ 🚏 ⛽ — Aéroport / Gare routière / Station Service

•• XIIth c — Site historique / XIIe siècle

🅐❶ 🄹 — Auberge(s) de pèlerins / Auberge de jeunesse / *CR* Incl. 35 € +

🄷 🄿 🄲 — Hôtel *H*° –*H*°°°° 30–90 € / Pension *P* 20 €+ / Chambre d'hôte

🄗 🄐 🄙 — *Hébergement hors itinéraire*

[32] — Nombre de places-lits (en général superposés)

[÷4]+ — ÷ nombre de dortoirs + *aussi des chambres privées*

Par. — Auberge de paroisse (don / 5 €)

Conv. — Auberge dans un couvent ou monastère (don / 5 € +)

Muni. — Auberge municipale 5 €

Xunta — Auberge du gouvernement *Xunta de Galicia* € 6

Asoc. — Auberge d'association € 7 / Incl. petit déjeuner compris

Priv. (*) — Auberge privée (réseau des auberges*) 10 € + / Incl.

Tous les prix sont approximatifs; à des fins de comparaison

▭ — Plan de ville

(Pop.–Alt. m) — Population - Altitude en mètres

▭ — Banlieue (gris)

▭ — Centre historique centro histórico (brun)

Introduction : Dans la vie de chacun de nous, il y a trop d'objets matériels. Dans le but d'alléger cette charge, nous avons créé une édition légère de cartes. Cela a été possible grâce au travail désintéressé des associations de pèlerins qui ont si bien marqué le parcours qu'aujourd'hui, pour atteindre la destination, on a simplement besoin de renseignements de base. Il est difficile de se perdre si on reste à tout moment concentré et attentif aux flèches jaunes indiquant Santiago : la clé, c'est la concentration. Prenez le temps de vous familiariser avec les symboles sur la page opposée.

La norme et le coût de l'hébergement pèlerin varie d'auberges *municipal* offrant des installations de base de 5 € (pas de réservation) à auberges privées à partir de € 10 + mais souvent avec des équipements supplémentaires tels que machines à laver et sécher. Une base repas de 3 plats avec du vin (Menú peregrino) coûte environ € 9

Ces cartes multilingues témoignent de la solidarité internationale du *Camino* qui favorise un sentiment de camaraderie et de fraternité, et d'une démarche spirituelle partagée qui est au cœur du pèlerinage. C'est ce qui distingue le pèlerinage de la grande randonnée.

Nous avançons tous en même temps sur deux voies : la voie externe, pour laquelle nous entrainons notre corps, et la voie interne qui correspond au voyage intérieur de l'âme. Nous devons être conscients de ces deux voies et prendre le temps de bien nous préparer. La tradition veut que le pèlerin chemine tout seul, à pied, portant ce qui lui est nécessaire pour le voyage. C'est la première leçon du pèlerin : laisser derrière soi tout le superflu et voyager avec seulement ce qui est nécessaire. La préparation pour le chemin interne est similaire : nous commençons par nous débarrasser des scories psychiques accumulées au fil des ans, comme les ressentiments, les préjugés et les systèmes de croyance dépassés. Avec un esprit et un cœur plus ouverts, on peut plus facilement assimiler les leçons que l'on tire le long de cette très ancienne voie de découverte.

Longtemps nous sommes restés endormis. Malgré le monde chaotique qui nous entoure, ou peut-être à cause de lui, il y a quelque chose qui nous travaille, et nous nous réveillons alors de notre amnésie collective. Un signe de cet éveil est le nombre de personnes qui sont attirées par les pèlerinages. Le rythme effréné de la vie moderne dont nous faisons l'expérience non seulement au travail, mais aussi dans notre vie familiale et sociale, nous propulse plus loin de notre centre. Nous nous sommes laissés projeter sur la surface de nos vies, en confondant celle-ci avec l'hyperactivité, mais cette existence superficielle n'est pas intrinsèquement satisfaisante.

Le pèlerinage nous donne l'occasion de ralentir le rythme et de donner une respiration à nos vies. Dans cet espace silencieux, on peut réfléchir sur le sens profond de notre existence et sur les raisons de notre présence sur terre. Le *Camino* nous incite à nous poser l'éternelle question : qui suis-je ? Et il nous donne le temps – ce qui est crucial – de comprendre et d'assimiler les réponses. Alors ne vous précipitez pas pour parcourir la route : prenez le temps nécessaire, car c'est peut-être le tournant de votre vie.

Quelle que soit la voie que vous choisissez, votre destination finale est la même. Le seul choix que vous ayez est le temps que vous prenez pour l'atteindre.

Buen camino.

Explicação das legendas dos mapas:

Total km	Distância total da etapa
	Ajustado para subida (100 m na vertical = mais 0,5 km)
(850m)**Alto▲**	Linha de relevo / Ponto mais alto da etapa
< Ⓐ Ⓗ >	Alojamento intermédio
◄ 3.5	Distância exacta entre pontos (3.5 km = ± 1 hora andar)
●150m > / ^ / <	Distâncias intermédias 150 metros virar à direita>
	/ seguir em frente^ / <virar à esquerda
⅏⅏⅏⅏ /⅏⅏⅏	Caminho ou carreiro (*verde*: caminho rural / *cinzento*: concreto)
⊜	Estrada secundária (*cinzento*: asfalto) / Rotunda
N-11	Estrada principal (*vermelho*: mais trânsito e perigo)
A-1	Auto-estrada (*azul*: cor convencional das auto-estradas)
+++++++●	Linha de trem / Estação ferroviária
● ● ● ● ●	Percurso principal (*amarelo*: ± 80% de todos os peregrinos)
● ● ● ● ●	Percurso rural alternativo (*verde*: mais afastado/menos peregrinos)
● ● ● ● ●	Desvio opcional para ponto de interesse (*turquesa*)
● ● ● ● ●	Percurso alternativo (*cinzento*: mais estradas – asfalto)
X **?** **!**	Cruzamento / Opção / Muito cuidado
⋔ ⋇ ⋏	Miradouro / Moinho/ Antena de transmissão
·—·/·—·	Fronteira nacional / Limite de província
~ / ~	Rio / Ribeiro
⬭ / ⬭	Estuário marítimo ou fluvial / Área florestal
♰ ♦ †	Igreja / Capela / Cruzeiro
⊕ ▬ ⊔	Fonte / Café-bar / Mini-mercado
menú *V.*	Menu peregrino ±€9 / *V.* Vegetariano
ℹ 🏠 ✗	Posto de turismo / Solar / Picnic
⊕ ⊕ ✉	Hospital / Farmácia / Posto de correios
⊕ 🚌 🅿	Aeroporto / Estação autocarros / Bomba gasolina
⁂ XII[th]c	Monumento histórico / Século 12
Ⓐ❶ **Ⓙ**	Albergue(s) de peregrinos / Pousada de juventude
Ⓗ **Ⓟ** **Ⓒ**	Hotel *H*˚–*H***** €30–90 / Pensão *P* €20+ / Casa rural *CR* €35+
Ⓗ Ⓐ Ⓙ	*alojamento perto mas fora*
[32]	Número de lugares (geralmente beliches)
[÷4]+	÷ numero de dormitórios + *quartos particulares*
Par.	Albergue parroquial doação / €5
Conv.	Albergue en un convento o monasterio doação / €5+
Muni.	Albergue municipal €5+
Xunta	Albergue de la Xunta de Galicia €6
Asoc.	Albergue a associação €7+
Priv. (*)	Alojamento privado (*Rede de Albergues) €10–15
	Os preços são aproximados e apenas a título de comparação.
▭	Planta da cidade
(Pop.–Alt. m)	População - altitude, em metros
▨	Subúrbios (*cinzento*)
	Centro histórico (*castanho*)

Introdução: Todos carregamos demasiados acessórios nas nossas vidas – num esforço para aliviar o peso produzimos este leve e fino volume de mapas básicos. Isto foi possível devido ao trabalho altruísta de organizações de apoio aos peregrinos que sinalizaram o Caminho de modo a que, hoje em dia, necessitemos de um mínimo de informações para nos levar ao destino. Será difícil perdermo-nos se nos mantivermos atentos às setas amarelas que indicam o caminho até Santiago.

O padrão e custo de alojamento peregrino varia de albergues municipais oferecendo facilidades básicas de 5 € (sem reserva prévia) para albergues privados a partir de € 10 +, mas geralmente com recursos adicionais, tais como máquinas de lavar e secar secadora. O último um benefício real em tempo de chuva. A 3 prato principal refeição básica com vinho (menu peregrino) a partir de 9 €.

Estes mapas multilingues reconhecem a irmandade internacional do Caminho. Espera-se que ajudem a forjar um sentido de camaradagem e comunhão – a partilha de uma intenção comum que está na base da peregrinação. É este objectivo transcendente que distingue uma peregrinação de uma mera caminhada.

Todos percorremos dois caminhos simultaneamente – o caminho exterior ao longo do qual transportamos o nosso corpo e um caminho interior, da alma. Devemos estar conscientes de ambos e encontrar o tempo de preparação adequada. A maneira tradicional do peregrino é viajar sozinho, a pé, carregando todas as possessões materiais necessárias para a viagem que tem pela frente. Isto proporciona a primeira lição do peregrino – deixar para trás tudo o que é supérfluo e viajar com o que é realmente necessário. A preparação para o caminho interior é semelhante – devemos começar por abandonar o lixo psíquico acumulado ao longo dos anos, os ressentimentos, os preconceitos e as crenças antiquadas. Com uma mente aberta poderemos assimilar mais facilmente as lições a tirar ao longo deste Caminho de Busca.

Há muito tempo que andamos adormecidos. Apesar do mundo caótico à nossa volta ou talvez por isso, algo está a compelir-nos para o despertar da nossa amnésia colectiva. Um sinal deste despertar é o número de pessoas atraídas pelo Caminho. O ritmo agitado da vida moderna, que sentimos tanto no nosso trabalho como na nossa vida familiar e social, atira-nos para longe de nós próprios. Deixámo-nos afastar para a periferia da nossa vida confundindo estar ocupado com estar vivo, mas esta existência superficial acaba por ser inerentemente insatisfatória.

A peregrinação oferece uma oportunidade de abrandar e dar amplitude à nossa vida. É nesse espaço mais calmo que se torna possível reflectir no significado mais profundo das nossas vidas e nas razões porque estamos aqui. O Caminho encoraja-nos a fazer a pergunta essencial – quem sou eu? E fundamentalmente dá-nos tempo para que as respostas sejam compreendidas e absorvidas. Portanto não apresse o Caminho – leve o tempo que precisar, ele pode-se tornar um ponto essencial de mudança na sua vida.

Buen camino.

Kaartsymbolen in deze handleiding:

Total km Totale afstand voor het aangegeven traject

Gecorrigeerd voor de klim (100m verticaal=0,5 km extra)

(850m) **Alto ▲** Contouren / Hoogste punt van elk traject

< A H > Accommodaties onderweg

◄ 3.5 Exacte afstand tussen twee punten(3,5 km= ongeveer 1uur wandelen)

●150m > / ^ / < Onderlinge afstand 150m rechts> / s/o recht door/ links<

........../......... Pad of spoor (*groen*: onverharde paden / *grijs*: verharde weg)

Secundaire weg (*grijs*: asfalt) / Rotonde

N-11 Hoofd(N-)weg (*rood*: extra verkeer en gevaar)

A-1 Autosnelweg (*blauw*: conventionele kleur)

++++++● Spoorweg / Station

X ? ǿ kruispunt / Optie / Extra oppassen

● ● ● ● ● Hoofdweg (*geel*: ong. 80% van de pelgrims)

● ● ● ● ● Verharde weg (*grijs*: meer asfalt)

● ● ● ● ● Schilderachtige route (*groen*: meer afgelegen / minder faciliteiten)

● ● ● ● ● Optionele omweg desvio naar bezienswaardigheid (*turqoise*)

✝ ☼ ✝ Windmolen / Uitkijkpunt / Zendmast

·—·/·—· Nationale grens / Provinciale grens

~/~ Rivier / Beek

◯/◯ Zee- of riviermonding / Bos

✝ ✝ ✝ Kerk / Kapel / Kruisbeeld langs de weg

ǿ ☕ ♨ Drinkwater / Café bar / kleine markt

menú *V.* Restaurant *menú peregrino* / Vegetarisch

🛈 🏠 ✕ Tourisme / Landhuis / Picknicktafel

✚ ✚ ✉ Apotheek / Ziekenhuis / Postkantoor

⊕ ☐ ▯ Vliegveld / Bus station / Tankstation

• • XIIth c Oud monument / 12th eeuw

A❶ **☐** Pelgrim hostel(s) / Jeugdherberg

H P C Hotel *H-H*****€30-90 / Pension *P**€20+ / B&B *CR* €35+ Incl.

Ⓗ Ⓐ Ⓙ *accommodaties buiten de route*

[32] Aantal slaapplaatsen (meestal stapelbedden)

[÷4]+ + aantal slaapzalen + ook privé kamers

Par. Kerk Parochie hostel Parroquia schenking *donativo* / €5

Conv. Convent of klooster hostel schenking *donativo* / €5

Muni. Gemeentelijk hostel €5+

Xunta Galician overheid Xunta de Galicia hostel €6

Asoc. Vereniging hostel €7+

Priv. (*) Particulier hostel (netwerk*) €10+ / Incl. inclusief ontbijt

Alle prijzen bij benadering; alleen voor vergelijkbare doeleinden

☐ Stadsplattegrond

(Pop.–Alt. m) (pop.—Alt.m) Inwoners-hoogte in meters

Voorsteden (*grijs*)

Historisch centrum centro historico (*bruin*)

Introductie: Ieder van ons heeft te veel ballast in zijn leven – in een poging om de last te verlichten, hebben wij een compacte uitgave van gidsen geproduceerd. Dit is mogelijk gemaakt door het onbaatzuchtige werk van pegrimsverenigingen die de route dusdanig gemarkeerd hebben, dat wij slechts zeer beperkt aanvullende informatie nodig hebben om onze bestemming te bereiken. Het zal moeilijk zijn om te verdwalen wanneer we aanwezig blijven in elk moment en aandachtig letten op de gele pijlen die de weg wijzen naar Santiago – bewuste aandacht is de sleutel. Neem de tijd om vertrouwd te raken met de kaartsymbolen op de pagina hiernaast.

De kwaliteit en kosten van pelgrim accommodaties variëren van parochie hostels op basis van donaties, gemeentelijke hostels die basis faciliteiten aanbieden voor € 5,00 (niet van tevoren te boeken) tot particuliere hostels vanaf €10,00 die over het algemeen extra faciliteiten bieden zoals wasmachines en drogers secadora. Dit laatste is een echte zegen bij regenachtig weer. Een standaard driegangenmenu met wijn is beschikbaar, menú peregrino, vanaf € 9,00.

Door deze meertalige gidsen herken je de internationale gemeenschap van de camino. Dit kan bijdragen aan een gevoel van samenhorigheid en kameraadschap; een gedeelde spirituele intentie die ten grondslag ligt aan de pelgrimage. Het is deze alle overstijgende intentie die de pelgrimage onderscheidt van een gewone langeafstandswandeling. We bevelen je aan om een gids te raadplegen met tips over hoe je je het beste kunt voorbereiden op een langere reis van deze aard, zoals het boek *A Pilgrim's Guide to the Camino Francés*, *een praktische & mystieke handleiding voor de moderne pelgrim (Engels).*

Ieder van ons bewandelt twee paden tegelijkertijd: de route die we fysiek bewandelen en het innerlijke pad van de ziel. We moeten aandacht hebben voor beiden en onzelf dienovereenkomstig voorbereiden. De traditionele manier van de pelgrim is alleen te reizen, te voet, met in je rugzak alleen die benodigdheden die je denkt nodig te hebben voor je reis. Dit biedt de eerste les voor de pelgrim – om al het overbodige achter te laten en alleen het hoogst noodzakelijke mee te nemen. Voorbereiding voor het innerlijke pad is vergelijkbaar – we beginnen bij het loslaten van psychische ballast die we in de jaren verzameld hebben, zoals ergernissen, vooroordelen en achterhaalde overtuigingen. Met een open geest en een open hart zullen we de lessen die geleerd kunnen worden langs het oude Spirituele Pad makkelijker in ons op kunnen nemen.

We zijn lange tijd in slaap gedut. Ondanks de chaotische wereld om ons heen, of misschien juist daardoor, heeft iets ons wakker geschud uit onze collectief geheugenverlies. Een teken van dit ontwaken is het aantal mensen dat zich aangetrokken voelt om de caminos te bewandelen. Het hectische tempo van het moderne leven, niet alleen ervaren in ons werk maar ook in ons gezins- en sociale leven, brengt ons verder weg van onze kern. We hebben onzelf toegestaan om oppervlakkig door het leven te gaan – daarbij drukte verwarrend met levendigheid, maar dit oppervlakkige bestaan is onvermijdelijk onbevredigend.

Pelgrimage biedt ons de mogelijkheid om te vertragen en wat ruimte toe te laten in ons leven. In deze stillere ruimte kunnen we reflecteren op de diepere betekenis van ons leven en de redenen van ons bestaan. De camino spoort ons aan om ons de eeuwige vraag te stellen – Wie ben ik? En cruciaal, het geeft ons tijd om de antwoorden te begrijpen en te integreren. Dus haast je niet op de camino – neem de tijd die het nodig heeft want het zou zomaar het cruciale keerpunt in je leven kunnen zijn.

Welke route we ook nemen, onze uiteindelijke bestemming staat vast. De enige keuze die we hebben is hoe lang we erover doen om te arriveren.

Buen camino.

Legenda do mapy używanej w tym przewodniku:

Total km — Całkowita odległość na mapie etapów

Dostosowanie do podejść (100 m w pionie=dodatkowe 0,5 km)

(850m) **Alto▲** — Profile / Najwyższy punkt każdego etapu

< 🏠 🏠 > — Noclegi pośrednia (często mniej zajęty / ciszej)

◀ **3.5** — Dokładna odległość między punktami (3,5 km = ± 1 godz.)

—•150m > / ^ / < — Odległości pośrednie •150 m skręt w prawo> / prosto^ /
                                 < w lewo

⊶⊶⊶ / ⊶⊶⊶ — Ścieżka lub szlak (*zielony*: ścieżka naturalna / *szary*: betonowa)

═══O═══ — Droga podrzędna (*szary*: asfalt) / Rondo

══**N-11**══ — Droga główna [N-] Nacional (*czerwony*: wzmożony ruch)

══**A-1**══ — Autostrada (*niebieski*: zwykłe autostrady)

++++++●● — Kolej ferrocarril / stacja estación

● ● ● ● ● — Trasa główna (*żółty*: ± 80% pielgrzymów)

● ● ● ● ● — Trasa krajobrazowa (*zielony*: dłuższa / mniej pielgrzymów)

● ● ● ● ● — Droga alternatywna (*szary*: więcej asfaltu)

● ● ● ● ● — Szlak alternatywny (*turkusowy*) do interesujących miejsc

X ? ⊖ — Skrzyżowanie *cruce* / Opcja *opción* / uwaga! *¡cuidado!*

🌫 ⬳ 🕴 — Wiatrak / Punkt widokowy / Maszt radiowy

▪—▪/▪—▪ — Granica państwa / Granica prowincji

~/~ — Rzeka / Potok

◯/◯ — Morze lub jezioro / Obszar leśny

🕆 🕈 ✝ — Kościół / kapliczka / Krzyż przydrożny

🅖 ☕ 🏪 — Źródło z wodą pitną / Kawiarnia / Sklep

menú V. — Menú peregrino obiad z trzech dań i wino / V. wegetariański

🅘 🏯 ✕ — Informacja turystyczna / Dwór / Miejsce piknikowe

⊕ ⊕ ✉ — Apteka / Szpital / Poczta

⊕ 🚏 🅿 — Lotnisko / Dworzec autobusowy / Stacja benzynowa

⁂ XII^thc — Zabytek / XII w.

🄰❶ 🄹 — Schronisko dla pielgrzymów / Schronisko młodzieżowe

🄷 🄿 🄲 — Hotel *H-H*""""€30-90 / Pensjonat *P*" €20+ / B&B *CR* €35+

🄷 🄰 🄹 — (zakwaterowanie poza trasą)

[32] — Liczba łóżek (zwykle łóżka piętrowe)

[÷4]+ — ÷ Liczba pokoi / + dodatkowe pokoje prywatne €20+

Par. — Ofiara za nocleg w parafii / €5

Conv. — Ofiara za nocleg w klasztorze / €5

Muni. — Schronisko miejskie €5+

Xunta — Schronisko należące do regionu Galicji *(Xunta hostel)* €6

Asoc. — Schronisko prowadzone przez stowarzyszenie €7+

Priv. (*) — Schronisko prywatne (sieciowe*) €10+ / ze śniadaniem
         Ceny podane są orientacyjnie; tylko dla porównania

▭ — Plan miasta z numerem strony

(Pop.–Alt. m) — Ludność miasta i położenie n.p.m. (w metrach)

▬ — Przedmieścia (*szary*)

Historyczne centrum *(brązowy)*

Wstęp: Wszyscy posiadamy zbyt dużo rzeczy: aby ulżyć w drodze, wydaliśmy ten skromny zbiór map. Było to możliwe dzięki bezinteresownej pracy stowarzyszeń pielgrzymów, które oznakowały szlaki tak, że obecnie potrzebujemy jedynie podstawowych informacji, aby dostać się do naszego celu. Byłoby to trudne, gdybyśmy stale wytężali uwagę na znalezienie wszystkich żółtych strzałek oznaczających drogę do Santiago – grunt to skupienie. Zapoznajcie się teraz z symbolami wykorzystanymi na mapach.

Wielojęzyczne mapy dowodzą istnienia międzynarodowej wspólnoty na Camino. Pomaga to rozwijać poczucie wspólnoty i braterstwa, budować wspólnotę duchową, która jest sercem pielgrzymowania. Ów niezwykły ogień odróżnia pątnika od turysty. Zalecamy zakup przewodnika ze wskazówkami, jak najlepiej przygotować się do takiej długiej wyprawy, jednego z polskich lub w poradnik *A Pilgrim's Guide to the Camino Francés*.

Wszyscy wędrujemy równocześnie dwiema ścieżkami: zewnętrzną, którą podąża nasze ciało i wewnętrzną drogą duszy. Trzeba być świadomym obydwu z nich i poświęcić czas na odpowiednie przygotowanie się. Tradycyjnym sposobem pielgrzymowania jest samotna wędrówka piesza i noszenie wszystkiego, czego potrzebujemy w drodze. To pierwsza lekcja dla pątnika: zostawić za sobą wszystko, co zbędne i podróżować jedynie z najbardziej potrzebnym wyposażeniem. Przygotowanie ścieżki wewnętrznej jest podobne: zaczynamy od pozostawienia wszelkich wewnętrznych „nieużytków" nagromadzonych przez lata, jak urazy, uprzedzenia i schematy myślowe. Otwartym umysłem i sercem łatwiej przyswoimy lekcje, które odnajdziemy na tej starej Drodze Doświadczenia.

Przez długi czas byliśmy pogrążeni w drzemce. Pomimo chaosu w otaczającym świecie albo raczej z jego powodu coś nas porusza, aby obudzić się z zapomnienia. Znakiem tego przebudzenia jest liczba ludzi, którzy są pociągani do wędrówki przez Camino. Pospieszne życie nowoczesnego świata nie tylko w naszej pracy, ale też w rodzinie i społeczeństwie, prowadzi nas na zewnątrz i pozostawia z dala od naszego wnętrza. Pozwoliliśmy się wyrzucić na powierzchnię naszego życia - myląc "bycie zajętym" z "byciem żywym". Ale ta powierzchowna egzystencja wcale nas nie cieszy.

Pielgrzymowanie daje okazję do tego, aby zwolnić i aby dać naszemu życiu trochę przestrzeni. W tej spokojniejszej przestrzeni możemy zastanowić się nad głębszym znaczeniem naszego życia i nad tym, po co istniejemy. Camino daje nam odwagę do zadawania nieprzemijających pytań: kim jestem? Oraz daje czas na odkrycie i zrozumienie odpowiedzi. A więc nie spieszcie się na Camino – dajcie sobie czas, jakiego wymaga, gdyż może stanowić punkt zwrotny w waszym życiu.

Którąkolwiek drogę wybierzemy, nasze ostateczne miejsce przeznaczenia jest pewne. Jedyny wybór, jakiego mamy dokonać, to czas, którego nam potrzeba, aby dotrzeć na *buen camino*.

ST. JEAN PIED de PORT *(pop. 1,800 – alt. 170m):*
Office de Tourisme © 0559 370 357 / © **France +33**

❑ **Monuments historiques:** *medieval rue de la Citadelle.* ❶ *Porte St Jacques XV* (UNESCO). ❷ *Citadelle (Table d'Orientation).* ❸ *La Maison des Evêques XVI.* ❹ *Porte de France* rue Eglise. ❺ *Porte de Navarre.* ❻ *Notre Dame du Bout du Pont XIV.* ❼ *Porte D'Espagne.*

■ **Pilgrim Passport:** *Carnet de Pelerin / Credencial* ■ *Accueil pèlerins* © 0559 370 509 *rue de la Citadelle (Nº39)* 07:30–12:30 / 13:30–22:00. **Pilgrim Equipment:** ■ *Boutique du pélerin (Nº32)* © 0559 379 852 / 06:30–19:00. **Backpack transfer & transport:** ■ *Express Burricot (Nº31)* © 0661 960 476 07:00–10:00 /16:30–20:30. Caroline Aphessetche www.expressbourricot.com

Porte Saint-Jacques
Albergue ❶ *Municipal*

■ *Albergues:* •*Rue de la Citadelle Nº55* ❶**Municipal** *[24÷3]* €10 incl. *Nº50* ❷**Azkorria** *Priv.[8÷2]*+ €16+ © 676 020 536. *Nº40* ❸**Bellari** *Priv.[18÷4]* €26 ½-b. © 0559 372 468. *Nº36* ❹**Au Chant du Coq** *Priv.[15]*+ © 0674 310 283. *Nº25* ❺**L'auberge du pèlerin** *Priv. [43÷4]* © 0559 491 086. *Nº8* ❻**Gite Ultreïa** *Priv.*[15÷4]*+ €16+€44 © 0680 884 622. •*Rue d'Espagne Nº21* (adj. L'Atelier du Chocolat) ❼**Le Chemin Vers L'Etoile** *Priv.[20÷5]* €15 incl. / €25 ½-b. © 0559 372 071. *Nº43* ❽**Maison Kaserna** *Par.[12÷1]* © 0559 376 517 €-donativo. *Outside the old town:* ●9 **Zuharpeta** *Priv.[22÷2]* © 0559 373 588 rue Zuharpeta 5. ●10 **Compostella** *Priv. [14÷2]* © 0559 370 236 rue d'Arneguy. ●11 **Refuge Esponda** *Priv.*© 0679 075 252 place du Trinquet €14.

■ *Hotels €60+:* H**Ramuntcho** © 0559 370 391 rue de Citadelle 24. *Gîte d'Étape* **Etchegoin** © 0559 371 208 Rue d'Uhart, 9. H**Les Remparts** © 0559 371 379 Place Floquet 16 & @Nº15 H**Etche Ona** © 0559 370 114. **Maison Ziberoa** © 661 235 944 route d'arnéguy 3. H**Central** Place du Général de Gaulle 1 © 0559 370 022. H**Itzalpea** © 0559 370 366 Place du Trinquet 5. H**Continental** © 0559 370 025 Av. Renaud (rue du Gare). *€120+H***Les Pyrénées** © 0559 370 101.

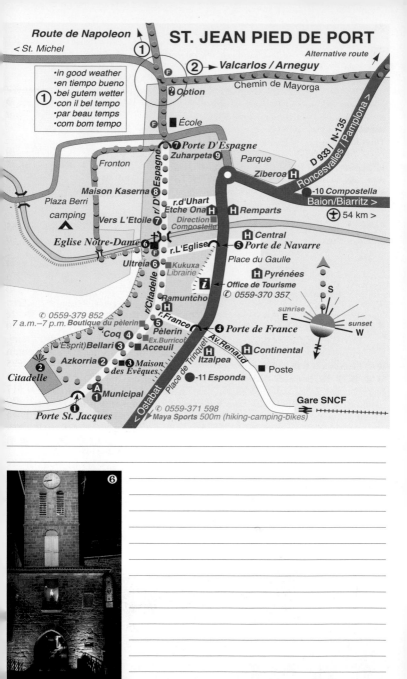

ST. JEAN PIED DE PORT

Route de Napoleon

< St. Michel

① Valcarlos / Arneguy

- in good weather
- en tiempo bueno
- **①** bei gutem wetter
- con il bel tempo
- par beau temps
- com bom tempo

Alternative route

Chemin de Mayorga

F

🚻 Option

F ■ École

❼ Porte D'Espagne
Zuharpeta **❾**

Parque

Ziberoa **H**

-10 Compostella
Baion/Biarritz >

Fronton

✚ 54 km >

Maison Kaserna **❽**

Plaza Berri

camping

r.d'Uhart
Etche Ona **H** **H** Remparts

Vers L'Etoile **❼**

Direction
Compostelle

Eglise Notre-Dame ■**❻** **F**

H Central

❺ Porte de Navarre

r.L'Eglise

Place du Gaulle

Ultreia **❻**

Kukuxa
Librairie

H Pyrénées

🛈 ← Office de Tourisme
© 0559-370 357

Ramuntcho

sunrise
S
E
sunset
W

H

r.France

© 0559-379 852
7 a.m.–7 p.m. Boutique du pèlerin

Coq **❹**

Pèlerin

❹ Porte de France

(L'Esprit)Bellari **❸**

Ex.Burricot
Acceuil

Azkorria **❷** ■ **❸** Maison

H Continental

Itzalpea

des Evêques

■ Poste

Citadelle

A

❶ Municipal

-11 Esponda

❶

Porte St. Jacques

© 0559-371 598
Maya Sports 500m (hiking-camping-bikes)

Gare SNCF
▬▬▬▬▬

Roncesvalles / Pamplona >
D 933 / N-135

01 778.5 km (483.7 ml) – Santiago de Compostela

ST. JEAN PIED-de-PORT (Pays Basque) – RONCESVALLES (Navarre)

⊓⊓⊓⊓⊓⊓⊓⊓⊓⊓	--- ---	12.4	--- --- *49%*
▬▬▬▬▬	--- ---	12.7	--- --- *51%*
	--- ---	0.0	
Total km	--- ---	**25.1** km (15.6 ml)	

32.0 km (^1,390m+6.9 km)
Alto ▲ Col de Loepeder 1,450m (4,757 ft)
< Ⓐ Ⓗ > Huntto **5.4** km – Orisson **7.8** km

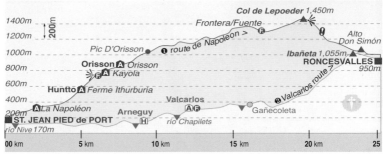

■ *℮ France + 33* ■ *℮ España + 34*
❶ ● ● ● ● *Route de Napoleón:* ■ **St. Jean Pied-de-Port:** D-428 Chemin de
Saint Jacques *Jondoni Jakobe Bidea. Alb.* **La Coquille Napoleón** *Priv.[10÷1]* €15
(menú €12) ℮ 0662 259 940. *Gite* **Villa Goxoki** ℮ 0559 491 773. ■ **Huntto:** *Alb.*
Ferme Ithurburia *Priv.[22÷4]+* ℮ 0559 371 117 €14 ½-b €32. ■ **Orisson:** *table*
d'orientation. Gite **Kayola** *Priv.[12]* €15 + *Auberge* **Orrison** *Priv.* [18÷3]* ℮ 0559
491 303 m: 681 497 956 – www.refuge-orisson.com ½-board €35. ❷ ● ● ● ●
Route de Valcarlos: **Areneguy:** *H°°* **Clementia** ℮ 0559 371 354. •*Café Venta Xabi.*
Valcarlos *Luzaide: Albergue* **Municipal** *[24÷2]* ℮ 646 048 883. *Hs°* **Maitena** ℮ 948
790 210. *Hs* **Casa Marcelino** ℮ 948 790 186. ■ **Roncesvalles** *Orreaga: Turismo* ℮
948 760 301. *Alb.* **Colegiata** *[183÷4]* €12 ℮ 948 760 000 + *credencial del peregrino*
10:00–22:00. *H°°°* **Roncesvalles** €60+ ℮ 948 760 105 **Casa de los Benficiados** €60+
menú. Hs **Casa Sabina** €40+ ℮ 948 760 012. *Hs* **La Posada** €45+ ℮ 948 760 225.

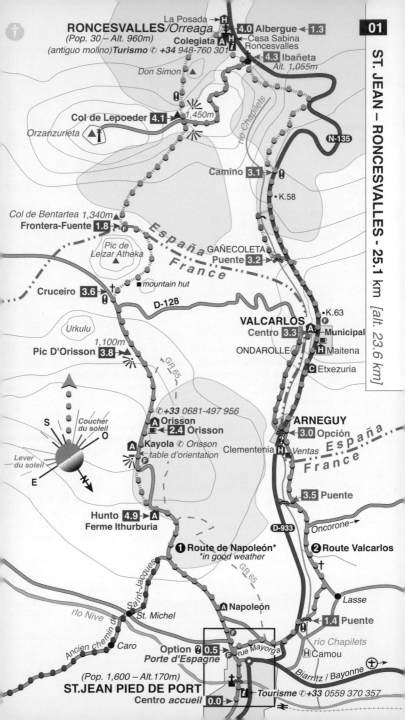

02 753.4 km (468.2 ml) – Santiago

RONCESVALLES – ZUBIRI

....	--- ---	17.5 --- ---	*80%*
―――	--- ---	3.2 --- ---	*15%*
▬▬▬	--- ---	1.2 --- ---	*5%*
Total km		**21.9** km (13.6 ml)	

◣◢ --- --- 23.1 km (^250m +1.2 km)

Alto ▲ Alto de Mezquíriz 955m (3,133 ft)

< Ⓐ Ⓗ > Burguete *Auritz* **3.1** km – Espinal *Aurizberri* **6.7** km.Viskarreta **11.8** km.

■ **Burguete** *Auritz:* Hs** **Burguete** €45+ ✆ 948 790 005. *CR* **Txikipolit** €25+ ✆ 948 760 019. Hs* **Iturrialdea** €25+ ✆ 948 760 243. Hs* **Jaundeaburre** ✆ 948 760 078. Hs* **Jauregui** ✆ 676 665 693. *P*² **Iturrialdea** ✆ 948 760 243. *CR* **Pedroarena** ✆ 948 760 164 c/ Berexi 6 €38. H*** **Loizu** €50 ✆ 948 760 008. •*Café Frontón* •*Panaderia La Borda.* **Espinal** *Aurizberri:* Alb. Hs **Haizea** *Priv.[30÷3]*+ €10 +€35 ✆ 948 760 379. Alb. **Irugoienea** *Priv.[18÷2]*+ €10 + ✆ 649 412 487. *CR* **Errebesena** ✆ 948 760 141. •*Café Keler.* ■ **Viscarreta** *Bizkarreta:* CR **Corazón Puro** €18 incl. ✆ 948 392 113. *CR* **La Posada Nueva** €25 ✆ 948 760 173. *CR* **Amatxi Elsa** €25 ✆ 948 760 391 c/ S.Pedro 14. *CR* **Maitetxu** €30 ✆ 948 760 175. •*Café Juan.* •*Supermercado*

■ **ZUBIRI:** *Alb.* ❶ **Río Arga Ibaia** *Priv.[8÷2]*+ €15-€40 ✆ 948 304 243. ❷ **Zaldiko** *Priv.[24÷3]* €10 ✆ 609 736 420. ❸ **El Palo de Avellano** *Priv.[40÷5]*+ €15-17 +€55. ✆ 948 304 770. ❹ **Segunda Etapa** *Priv.[12÷2]* €15 ✆ 697 186 560. ❺ **Escuela** *Muni.[48÷2]* €4-8 Av. Zubiri *[+300m].* ❻ **Suseia** *Priv.[22÷4]*+ €15 ✆ 948 304 353 c/ Murelu, 12 *[+500m].* P* **Zubiaren Etxea** ✆ 948 304 293. P* **Usoa** ✆ 628 058 048. P* **Amets** ✆ 948 304 308. **N-135:** P* **Goika** ✆ 638 847 974. P* **Benta Berri** ✆ 636 134 781. Hs* **Zubiri** €60-€110 ✆ 948 304 329. Hs **Gau-Txori** €40 ✆ 948 30 45 31 Av Roncesvalles, 24. •*Bar Valentin* •*Café Ogi Berri.*

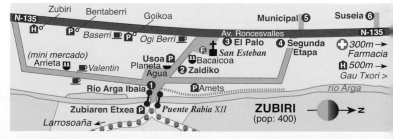

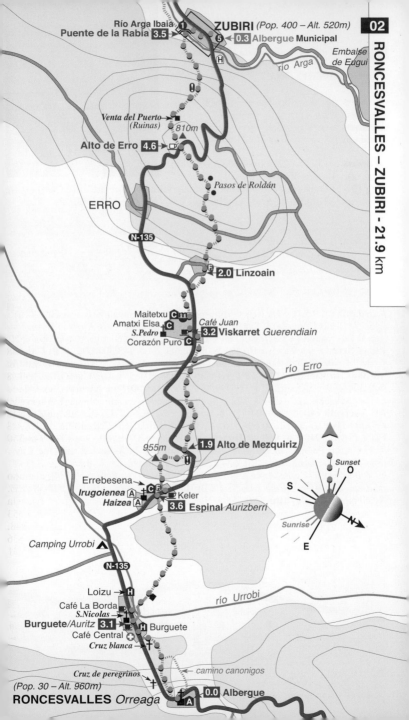

ZUBIRI *(Pop. 400 – Alt. 520m)*

Río Arga Ibaia **1**
Puente de la Rabia **3.5**

5 ◄ **0.3** Albergue **Municipal**

H

río Arga

Embalse de Eugui

Venta del Puerto →
(Ruinas)

810m

Alto de Erro **4.6** ▢

Pasos de Roldán

ERRO

N-135

2.0 **Linzoain**

Maitetxu **C** m
Amatxi Elsa **C** *Café Juan*
S.Pedro **3.2** **Viskarret** *Guerendiain*
Corazón Puro **C**

río Erro

955m **1.9** **Alto de Mezquiriz**

Errebesena
Irugoienea **A** **C** F
Haizea **A** Keler
3.6 **Espinal** *Aurizberri*

Camping Urrobi ▲

N-135

río Urrobi

Loizu **H**
Café La Borda
S.Nicolas →
Burguete/ *Auritz* **3.1** **H** Burguete
Café Central ✚
Cruz blanca → †

Cruz de peregrinos ← *camino canonigos*
†
(Pop. 30 – Alt. 960m)
RONCESVALLES *Orreaga*
A **0.0** Albergue

Sunset
O
S
N
Sunrise
E

03 731.5 km (454.5 ml) – Santiago

ZUBIRI – PAMPLONA

⫶⫶⫶⫶⫶⫶ --- ---	13.3 --- ---	64%
▬▬▬ --- ---	2.2 --- ---	11%
▬▬▬ --- ---	5.4 --- ---	25%
Total km	**20.9** km (13.0 ml)	

◣◣ --- --- 22.7 km (^360m + 1.8 km)

Alto ▲ Ilarratz 560m (1,837 ft)

< Ⓐ Ⓗ > Larrasoaña *(+0.3)* **5.3** km – Zuriain **9.1** km – *[Zabaldika 12.7 km (+0.3)]* - Trinidad de Arre / Villalba **16.1** km – *[Huarte 16.6 km].*

■ **Urdániz** *(+ 0.5 km) Hs* **Acá y Allá** *Priv.[6÷1]* €15 / menú €10 + piscina ✆ 615 245 439 (Jesús Góngora) c/ San Miguel 18. ■ **Larrasoaña:** *Café Taberna Perutxena. Alb.* ❶ **Larrasoaña** *Muni.[60÷8]* €6 ✆ 605 505 489 c/San Nicolás (Concello). ❷ *Hs* **Bide Ederra** *Priv.[4÷1]+* €16+40 c/San Nicolás 27 ✆ 948 304 692. *P* ̊ **El Camino** *Casa Sangalo* €60 ✆ 948 304 250 + *bar/ restaurant menú. P* **Tau** €60 ✆ 948 30 4 720 c/ Errotabidea 18. *P* ̊ **El Peregrino** ✆ 948 304 554. *CR* **Casa Elita** €60 ✆ 948 304 449 c/ Amairu 7 + •*Comercio Casa Elita.* ❸ **San Nicolás** *Priv.[40÷8]* €11 ✆ 619 559 225 (Luis y María Jesús) + •*Supermercado Amari.* ■ **Akerreta:** *H* ̊ ̊ ̊ **Akerreta** €80 ✆ 948 304 572. ■ **Zuriáin:** *Alb. & Café* **La Parada de Zuriain** *Priv.[4÷1]+* €16-20 incl. ✆ 699 556 741. ● **Zabaldika:** *Alb.* **Zabaldika** *Par.[18÷2]* €-donativo ✆ 948 330 918. ● **Huarte:** *Alb.* **Huarte** *Muni.[60÷7]* €10 ✆ 948 334 413. ■ **Arre** *Puente río Ultzama: Alb.* **Cofradía de la Trinidad de Arre** *Conv. [34÷4]* € 8 *Hermanos Maristas* ✆ 948 332 941. ■ **Villava** *Alb.* **Villava** *Muni.[48÷5]* €9 ✆ 948 331 971 c/Pedro de Atarrabia [+200m]. *P* **Etxea** ✆ 696 597 140 c/ grupo martiket, 6 [+400m]. *Café Paradiso.* ■ **Burlada** *H* ̊ **La Buhardilla** ✆ 948 382 872 Av. Serapio Huici. *H* ̊ ̊ **Burlada** ✆ 948 333 676 c/Fuente.

PAMPLONA
(Pop. 200,000)

Turismo © 848 420 420 ℹ️

Catedral **1.0**

3.8 Puente *Magdalena*

A-15

"Bienvenida Pamplona" Lagun Artea

→ *Jardineria Arvéna*

BURLADA

Puente Viejo Burlada →
La Buhardilla

Ⓗ Burlada

VILLAVA

PA-30

Pasarela

Molino S.Andrés

Municipal Villava

HUARTE
Huarte Municipal Ⓐ

Ⓐ

Ⓐ **3.7** **Trinidad de Arre Cofradía**

Miravalles

río Ulztama

→ *Túnel*

Parque Fluvial
Riverside Walk

†*Arleta*

Monte
Nerval

Túnel →

N-121

río Ulzama

ZABALDIKA
S.Esteban XII–XVII

Opción 3.3 → Ⓐ **Parroquia**

Puente de Iturgaiz →

IROTZ
Horno Irotz ■

▲ *770m*
Armiñagain

ZURIÁIN

Café La Parada → Ⓐ **La Parada**
Puente de Zuriain 3.8 →

río Arga

AKERRETA Ⓗ **Hotel Akerreta**

Ⓐ

Puente 5.3 **LARRASOAÑA**
(Pop. 200)

ESQUIROZ Ⓕ

Abadia XII †
ILLARATZ Ⓕ

Ⓐ *Acá y Allá* (+ 0.5 km)

O
la puesta del sol

S

la salida del sol

E

Ostériz

■ ← **Magna** *(Magnesitas Navarras)*

N-135

Puente *de Rabia* **0.0** → Ⓐ **ZUBIRI**

PAMPLONA pop. 200,000 (Codex Calixtinus III).
❏ *Turismo*, Av. Roncesvalles, 4 ✆ 848 420 420 (10.00-17.00 / 10.00-14.00).
❏ *Caminoteca* c/Curia, 15 ✆ Itsván & Anita 948 210 316.

❶ **Puente de Magdalena** *XII.* ❷ **Portal de Francia** *(Zumalacárregi)* ● **Baluarte del Redín** *rincón y cruz de Menidero.* ❸ **Catedral de Santa María la Real** *XV Claustro / Puerta Preciosa / Diocesan museu (€2 + credencial).* ● **Plaza de Toros** Paseo Ernest Hemingway. ● **S. Bartolomé Fortín** *XVII.* ● **Plaza del Castillo.** ❹ **Iglesia San Nicolás** *XII* c/San Nicolás & c/San Miguel. ❺ **San Saturnino** *(San Cernín) XIII* ❻ **Casa Consistorial** *(encierros).* ❼ **Museo de Navarra** c/Santo Domingo. ❽ **Iglesia San Lorenzo** *(y Capela de San Fermín).* ❾ **Ciudadela.**

▮ *Albergues Centro:* ❶ **Casa Paderborn** *Asoc.[26÷5] €9* ✆ *948 211 712 Playa de Caparroso, 6.* ❷ **Ibarrola** *Priv.[20÷1]* €18 incl. ✆ 948 223 332 c/ Carmen, Nº31 @Nº18 ❸ **Iruñako Aterpea** *Priv.[22÷1]* €14 ✆ 948 044 637. ❹ **Jesús y María** *Asoc.[114÷2]* €7 ✆ 948 222 644 *Iglesia Jesús y María XVII* c/ Compañía. ❺ **Plaza Catedral** *Priv.[46÷5]* €15-18 ✆ 948 591 336 c/ Navarrería 35. ❻ **Ciudadela 7** *Priv. [24÷4]* €16 ✆ 616 786 479 c/Ciudadela 7, 1º. ▮ *Hostels:* (€15+): ● **Hemingway** c/ Amaya,26 ✆ 948 983 884. ● **Aloha** c/Sangüesa,2 ✆ 648 289 403. ● **Xarma** Av. Baja Navarra ✆ 948 046 449. ● **Juvenil** *youth hostel* c/Goroabe, 36. ▮ *Hoteles:* (€35-€55) *P** **Lambertini** c/Mercadore, 17 ✆ 948 210 303. *P* **La Viña** c/Jarauta, 8 ✆ 948 213 250. *P* **Eslava** c/Eslava, 13 ✆ 948 221 558. *P* **Escaray** c/Nueva, 24 ✆ 948 227 825. *Calle San Nicolás:* *P*** **Otano** ✆ 948 227 036 @Nº5. *P** **San Nicolás** ✆ 948 221 319 @Nº13. *Hs* **Don Lluis** ✆ 948 210 499 @Nº24. *Hs* **Aralar** ✆ 948 221 116 @Nº12. *Calle San Gregorio:* *P** **La Montañesa** @Nº2 ✆ 948 224 380. *P** **Dionisio** @Nº 5 ✆ 948 224 380. *P** **El Camino** @Nº 12 ✆ 638 206 664. *Hs*** Hotel **Eslava** Plaza Virgen de la O *(Parque Traconera).* *Avenida Pio XII.* *P** **Payvi II / III** ✆ 948 278 508 @Nº30. *P** **Pasadena** ✆ 948 177 650 @Nº32. *H**** **Hotel Blanca de Navarra** @Nº43 ✆ 948 171 010. *Hoteles:* (€70+) *H***** **Iruña Palace Tres Reyes** ✆ 948 226 600. *H****** **La Perla** ✆ 948 223 000 Plaza del Castillo. *H***** **Pamplona Catedral** ✆ 948 226 688 c/ Dos de Mayo (< *Puerta del camino / Convento).*

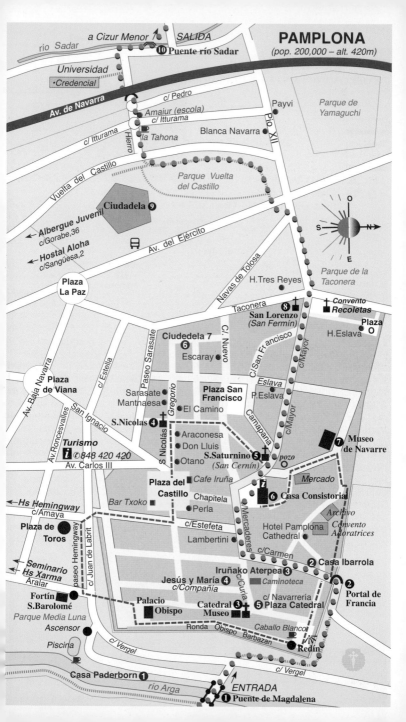

04 **710.6** km (441.5 ml) – Santiago

PAMPLONA – PUENTE LA REINA

····················	--- ---	16.6	--- ---	70%
	--- ---	4.1	--- ---	17%
	--- ---	3.1	--- ---	13%
Total km		**23.8** km	(14.8 ml)	

▲ --- --- 25.5 km (+1.7 km)
Alto ▲ Alto de Perdón 790m (2,590 ft)
< 🅰 🅗 > Cizur Menor **5.0** km – Zariquiegui **11.1** km – Uterga **17.3** km – Muruzábal **19.8** km – Óbanos **21.6** km.

[Elevation profile]
Alto del Perdón 750m
700m
600m
Zariquiegui 🅰
500m Cizur Menor 🅰 Uterga 🅰 Óbanos
■ PAMPLONA Muruzábal 🅲
400m río Sadar PUENTE LA REINA
río Arga ▼■
300m
00 km   5 km   10 km   15 km   20 km

❚ **Cizur Menor:** Iglesia de San Miguel Arcángel *XII. Alb.* ❶ **Sanjuanista** *Priv. [27÷3]* €4 ☎ 616 651 330 Orden de San Juan de Malta. *Alb.* ❷ **Roncal** *Priv.[50÷5]* €10 Maribel Roncal ☎ 670 323 271. ● ***Cizur Mayor*** *Zizur Maior: (+1.5 km).* H **Casa Azcona** Av. Belascoaín ☎ 948 287 662. *H****AC **Zizur Mayor** ☎ 948 287 119. *Hs* **Nekea** ☎ 948 185 044 Travesia S.Francisco. ❚ **Zariquiegui:** *Albergue.* ❶ **San Andrés** *Priv.[18÷2]* €10 ☎ 948 353 876 + •*Café*. ❷ **La Posada de Ardogi** *Priv. [16÷2]* €11 ☎ 948 353 353. ❚ **Uterga:** *Alb.* ❶ **Municipal** *[2÷1].* ❷ **Camino del Perdón** *Priv.[16÷1]*+ €10 + ☎ 948 344 598 + •*Café menú.* ❸ **Casa Baztán** *Priv. [24÷1]*+ €10 + €45 ☎ 948 344 528 m: 691 840 408 c/Mayor 46. ❚ **Muruzábal**: *Alb.* ❶ **El Jardín** *Priv.[14÷1]*+ €10-€50 ☎ 696 688 399 c/ Monteviejo 21. ❷ **Mendizabal** *Priv.[10÷4]* €18 incl. ☎ 948 344 169 c/ Mayor 7. *CR* **Villazón II** ☎ 630 767 346. *Bar/restaurant Nogales.* ●***Eunate:*** *(+2.4 km)* Iglesia Santa María de Eunate *XII.* ❚ **Óbanos:** *Alb.* **Usda** *Priv.[36÷3]* €8 ☎ 676 560 927 c/San Lorenzo. *Hs* **Mamerto** €30-45 ☎ 948 344 344 c/San Lorenze 13. *CR* **Villazón II** €35-50 ☎ 620 441 467. *CR* **Raichu** €30-45 ☎ 948 344 285 c/ Larrotagaña 2.

Santa María de Eunate

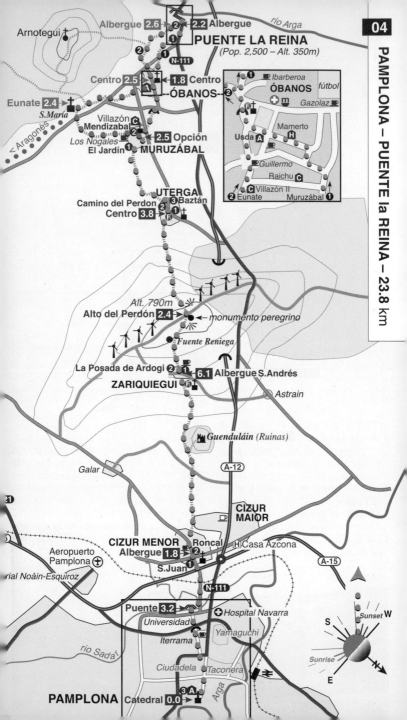

Albergue **2.6** → **2.2** Albergue
río Arga

PUENTE LA REINA
(Pop. 2,500 – Alt. 350m)
N-111

■ Ibarberoa
ÓBANOS   fútbol
Gazolaz

Centro **2.5**   **1.8** Centro
ÓBANOS

Mamerto

Eunate **2.4** →
S.María
Usda

< Aragonés
Villazón
Mendizabal
Guillermo

2.5 Opción
Los Nogales
Raichu
El Jardín
MURUZÁBAL
Villazón II
Eunate   Muruzábal

UTERGA
3 Baztán
Camino del Perdón
Centro **3.8**

Alt. 790m
Alto del Perdón 2.4 → ← *monumento peregrino*

Fuente Reniega

La Posada de Ardogi **2** **1** **6.1** Albergue S.Andrés
ZARIQUIEGUI
Astrain

Guenduláin (Ruinas)

Galar
A-12

CIZUR MAIOR

CIZUR MENOR Roncal H.Casa Azcona
Albergue **1.8** → **2**
Aeropuerto
Pamplona ⊕
S.Juan
A-15
rial Noáin-Esquiroz
N-111

Puente **3.2**
✚ Hospital Navarra
Universidad
Iterrama   *Yamaguchi*
río Sadar
Ciudadela   Taconera

PAMPLONA Catedral **0.0**   **3 A**   Arga

S   Sunset W
Sunrise
E

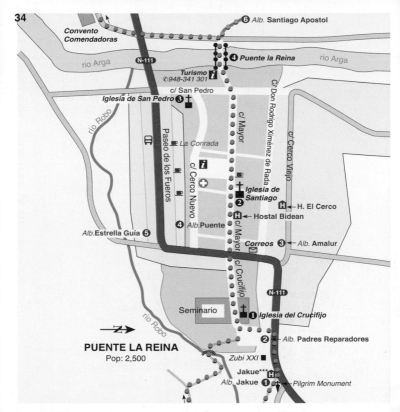

❑ **PUENTE LA REINA:** Tourist office ✆ 948 341 301 c/ Mayor (Puente).
❚ **Hostales:** *Alb.* ❶ **Jakue** *Priv.*[40÷2]*+ €10 / *menú peregrino* €13 ✆ 948 341 017. *H**** **Jakue** €45. ❷ *Alb.* **Padres Reparadores** *Conv.[96÷10]* €5 ✆ 948 340 050 c/ Crucifijo. *Alb.* ❸ **Amalur** *Priv.[20÷2]* €12 incl. ✆ 948 341 090. c/Cerco Viejo. ❹ **Puente** *Priv.[22÷3]*+ €12 incl (+€34) ✆ 661 705 642 Paseo de los Fueros,57 / c/ Cerco Nuevo,57. ❺ **Estrella Guía** *Priv.[6÷2]* €12 incl. ✆ 948 340 001 Paseo de Los Fueros, 34 / 2º piso. ❻ **Santiago Apostol** *Priv.* [100÷5]* €8 ✆ 948 340 220.
❚ **Hoteles:** *H* **Bidean** ✆ 948 341 156 c/Mayor from €50. *H* **El Cerco** ✆ 948 34 12 69 €60 c/Rodrigo Ximenez de Rada. + *H* **Jakue** ❑ **Monumentos:** ❶ *Iglesia del Crucifijo (Crucifijo XIV).* ❷ *Iglesia de Santiago (Peregrino Beltxa XII).* ❸ *Iglesia San Pedro Apóstol (N.S del Puy / Txori).* ❹ *Puente la Reina (Doña Mayor).*

Ayegui

❻

❺ Oncineda

N-111

ESTELLA
(LIZARRA)
(pop. 14,000 – alt. 425m)

Capuchinos
Rocamador ❹

c/Mon...

Río Ega

*Parque
de los Llanos*

Cruz de los Castillo

*Convento de
San Benito*

*Convento de
Santa Clara
s.XVII*

c/San Nicolás

Túnel

San Pedro ❹

Santo
Domingo

Aljama

Turismo © 948 556 301

i

Estación de Autobuses

Hospital de
Peregrinos

❶

❸ Palacio/Museo

Sancho el Sabio

c/Rúa

❷ **S.Martín**

N-111

❶ Puente Carcel

Correos

Paseo de la Inmaculada

c/Alda - c/Zapateria

c/Mayor

❺ **Chapitel**

San Miguel

San Juan

Cristina

San Andres

c/Mayor

Plaza
Fueros

Casanova

Plaza Santiago

ANFAS

❸

Mercado Viejo

Guardia Civil

San Miguel ❷

*Gebala
Apartamentos*

❻

Yerri

Izarra

San Benito *(Convento Benedictinas)*
Basílica del Puy

❏ **ESTELLA:** *Turismo:* © 948 556 301 c/ San Nicolas / Plaza de San Martin.
▮ **Albergues: ❶ Hospital Peregrinos** *Asoc.[96÷5]* €6 © 948 550 200 c/La Rúa, 50.
❷ San Miguel *Par.[32÷2]* €-donativo © 615 451 909 cMercado Viejo, 18 **❸ ANFAS**
Mun.[34÷1] €7 © 639 011 688 c/Cordeleros, 7 Bajo. **❹ Rocamador** *Conv.[28÷5]+*
€15-18 +€40 © 948 550 549 Hermanos Capuchinos c/ Rocamador 6 *(capilla virgen
de Rocamador XII).* **❺** *Juvenil* **Oncineda** *Muni.[150÷20]* €9–13 © 948 555 022.
❻ San Cipriano de Ayegui *Mun.[80÷2]* © 948 554 311 c/Polideportivo, Ayegui.

▮ **Hostales:** *Hospederia* **Convento Benedictinas** Monasterio San Benito (Basilica
del Puy). *P* **San Andrés** €39+ © 948 554 158 plaza de Santiago. *Hs* **Cristina** €40
© 948 550 450 c/Baja Navarra 1 / c/Mayor. *P* **Fonda Izarra** €20-40 © 948 550 678
c/Caldería 20. *P* **Apartamentos Gebala** €50 © 606 980 675 plaza Fueros, 31. *H****

Chapitel €70+ © 948 551 090 c/Chapitel.
Hs **El Volante** €40+ © 948 553 957 c/
Merkatondoa + *Hs* **Area-99** © 948 553
370. *H*** **Yerri** €45-€65 © 948 546 034.
❏ **Monumentos: ❶** *Puente de Carcel.* **❷**
*Plaza San Martín Fuente de los Chorros
XVI.* **❸** *Palacio de los Reyes de Navarra
XII y museo.* **❹** *San Pedro de la Rúa y
Claustro XII.* **❺** *Iglesia San Miguel.* **❻**
Iglesia de San Juan Bautista.

05 **686.8** km (426.7 ml) – Santiago

PUENTE LA REINA – ESTELLA (Navarra)

⊪⊪⊪⊪⊪⊪⊪	--- ---	16.5	--- ---	*75%*
▬▬▬▬	--- ---	5.4	--- ---	*25%*
▬▬▬▬	--- ---	0.0		
Total km		**21.9** km (13.6 ml)		

◣◣ --- --- 23.4 km (^300m + 1.5 km)

Alto ▲ Ciraqui 500m (1,640 ft)

<🏠 🏨> Mañeru **5.2** km – Ciraqui **7.8** km – Lorca **13.5** km – Villatuerta **18.0** km.

▌Mañeru: *Alb.* ❶ **Lurgorri** *Priv.[12÷1]* €10 incl. ☎ 686 521 174 c/Esperanza, 5 & @ Nº2 ❷ **El Cantero** *Priv.[26÷2]* €10 ☎ 948 342 142 Roberto. *CR* **Isabel** ☎ 948 340 283. **▌Ciraqui:** (*Zirauki*) *Café El Portal*. Iglesia San Román *XIII* y *Santa Catalina*. *Alb.* ❶ *Par.[14÷1]* €-*donativo*. ❷ **Maralotx** *Priv.[28÷3]*+ €11 ☎ 678 635 208. **▌Lorca:** *Alb.* ❶ **La Bodega del Camino** *Priv.[30÷5]*+ ☎ 948 541 327 c/Mayor opp: *Alb.* ❷ **Lorca** *Priv.[12÷3]*+ ☎ 948 541 190. *Cafe Casa Julio* **▌Villatuerta:** *Alb.* **Villatuerta** *Casa Mágica Priv.**[42÷5]*+ ☎ 948 536 095 c/ Rebote, 5. *Iglesia de la Anunciación XIV*.

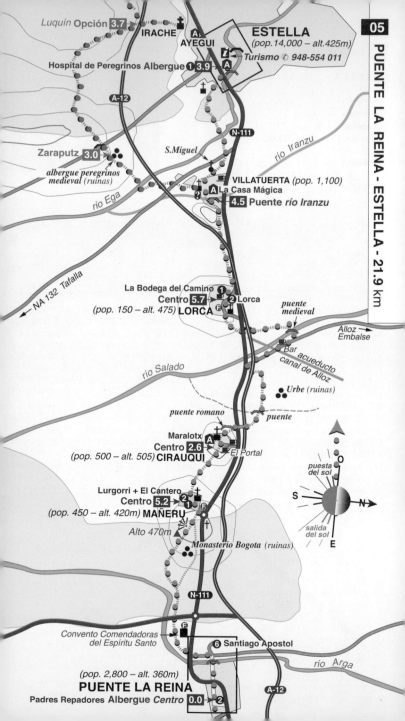

Luquín Opción **3.7**
IRACHE

A
AYEGUI

ESTELLA
(pop. 14,000 – alt. 425m)
Turismo © 948-554 011

A-12

Hospital de Peregrinos Albergue **1** **3.9**

A

Zarapuz 3.0

albergue peregrinos medieval (ruinas)

S. Miguel

río Iranzu

N-111

río Ega

VILLATUERTA *(pop. 1,100)*
A **La Casa Mágica**
4.5 **Puente** *río Iranzu*

NA 132 Tafalla

La Bodega del Camino **1**
Centro 5.7 **2** **Lorca**
(pop. 150 – alt. 475)
LORCA

puente medieval

Alloz →
Embalse

río Salado

Bar *acueducto canal de Aloz*

● *Urbe (ruinas)*

puente romano

puente

Maralotx
A
Centro 2.6
(pop. 500 – alt. 505) **CIRAUQUI**
El Portal

Lurgorri + El Cantero
Centro 5.2 **1** **2**
(pop. 450 – alt. 420m) **MAÑERU**

Alto 470m

Monasterio Bogota (ruinas)

N-111

puesta
del sol

O

S ——— N

salida
del sol

E

Convento Comendadoras del Espíritu Santo

6 **Santiago Apostol**

río Arga

(pop. 2,800 – alt. 360m)
PUENTE LA REINA
Padres Repadores Albergue *Centro* **0.0** **2**

A-12

06 **664.9** km (413.2 ml) – Santiago

ESTELLA – LOS ARCOS (Navarra)

....	--- ---	17.5 --- ---	82%
	--- ---	3.7 --- ---	17%
	--- ---	0.3 --- ---	1%
Total km		**21.5** km (13.4 ml)	

--- --- 23.3 km (^370m + 1.8 km)

Alto ▲ Monjardín 690m (2,132 ft)

< **Ⓐ Ⓗ** > Ayegui **1.5** km – Hotel Irache **4.0** km – Monjardín **9.3** km.

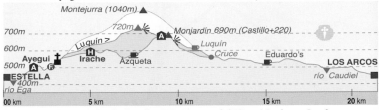

■ **Irache: Monasterio de Irache** *XII. Fuente del Vino / Bodegas Irache y museo.* *H******Lur Gorri** *Irache* €50+ *©* 948 558 286 + **camping** (chalet €28+). ■ **Azqueta:** *Alb.* **La Perla Negra** *Priv.[9÷3]*+ €27 incl.menú *©* 627 114 797 c/Carrera,18. ■ **Villamayor de Monjardín:** *Alb.* **❶ Villamayor** *Priv.[20÷3]*+ €15 incl. (+€40) *©* 677 660 586. **❷ Hogar** *Asoc.[25÷5]* €5 (menú €10) *©* 948 537 136. *CR* **Montedeio** €35-55 *©* 948 551 521 c/ Mayor, 17. ■ **LOS ARCOS:** *Alb.* **❶ la Fuente** *Priv. [48÷6]*+ €8 + *©* 948 640 797. **❷ Casa de la Abuela** Priv.*[24÷2]*+ €9 (+€35) *©* 948 640 250 adj. Plaza de Santa Maria. **❸ Isaac Santiago** *Muni.[72÷8]* €6 *©* 948 441 091 c/ El Hortal. **❹ Casa Alberdi** *Priv.[24÷3]* €10 *©* 948 640 764. *P* **Ostadar** €30 *©* 649 961 440 c/ San Lázaro 9 adj. Alberdi. *Apt.* **Capuchinos** €20+ *©* 665 954 824 c/Capuchinos 1. *P* **Mavi** *©* 948 640 081 c/del Medio,7. *H*** **Mónaco** *©* 948 640 000 €40 Plaza del Coso. *Hs* **Suetxe** €60 *©* 948 441 175 c/Karramendabia. *Hs* **Ezequiel** €26+ *©* 948 640 296 c/La Serna. *[**Mués** +5 km (transporte gratuito © 948 441 152) H rural **Latorrién de Ane** €70-180 incl. c/ mayor 128.]* ❏ **❶ Iglesia de Santa María de los Arcos** *XII.* **❷ Portal de Castilla.** **❸ Casa del Coso** *XVI* (*Turismo / Balcón de Toros*). **❸ Ayutamiento** *XVI.*

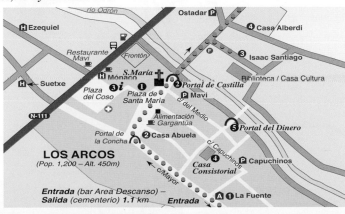

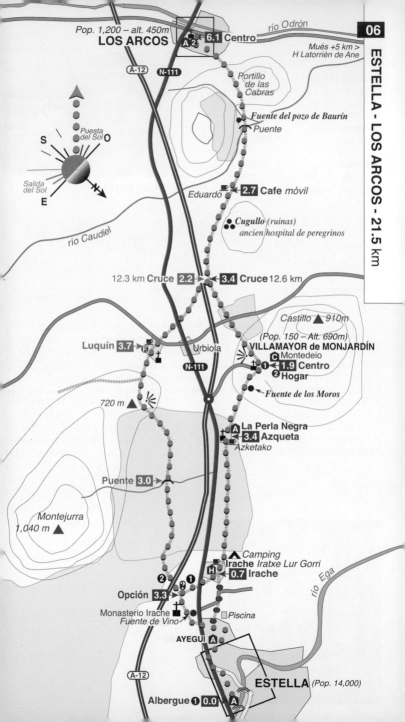

Pop. 1,200 – alt. 450m
LOS ARCOS 🏨 2 6.1 Centro

río Odrón

Mués +5 km >
H Latorrién de Ane

(A-12) N-111

Portillo de las Cabras

Fuente del pozo de Baurín
← Puente

Puesta del Sol O
S
Salida del Sol N
E

río Caudiel

Eduardo 2.7 **Cafe** *móvil*

*Cugullo (ruinas)
ancien hospital de peregrinos*

12.3 km **Cruce** 2.2 → ← 3.4 **Cruce** 12.6 km

Castillo ▲ 910m

(Pop. 150 – Alt. 690m)
VILLAMAYOR de MONJARDÍN
C Montedeio
Luquín 3.7 → F
Urbiola
N-111
1 1.9 Centro
2 Hogar

Fuente de los Moros

720 m ▲

A **La Perla Negra**
3.4 **Azqueta**
Azketako

Puente 3.0 →

*Montejurra
1,040 m* ▲

▲ *Camping*
Irache *Iratxe Lur Gorri*
H 0.7 **Irache**

río Ega

2 1
Opción 3.3 →
Monasterio Irache
Fuente de Vino
🔲 *Piscina*

AYEGUI A

ESTELLA *(Pop. 14,000)*

Albergue 1 0.0 A

07 **643.4** km (399.8 ml) – Santiago

LOS ARCOS – LOGROÑO

Navarra	*La Rioja*			
ⅲⅲⅲⅲⅲⅲⅲ	--- ---	18.4	--- ---	*66%*
▬	--- ---	8.3	--- ---	*30%*
▬▬	--- ---	<u>1.1</u>	--- ---	*4%*
Total km		**27.8** km	(17.3 ml)	

▲▬ --- --- 29.3 km (+1.5 km)
Alto ▲ N. Sra. del Poyo 570m (1,870 ft)
<🅐 🅗> Sansol **6.8** km – Torres del Río **7.8** – Viana **18.4** km.

Profile diagram:
- 600m — Alto N.S. del Poyo 570m
- 500m — Sansol 🅐 🚶 — Viana 🅐 — Alto Cantabria
- ▬LOS ARCOS — 🅐 Torres —
- 400m — río S.Pedro — río Linares — río Cornava — río Labraza — LOGROÑO▬
- 300m — río Ebro
- 00 km — 5 km — 10 km — 15 km — 20 km — 20 km

▐ **Sansol:** *Alb.* **Sansol** *Priv.[24÷1]* €10 / menú €8 ✆ 948 648 473 c/ Barrio Nuevo 4. *CR* **El Olivo de Sansol** €25+ incl. ✆ 948 648 345. ▐ **Torres del río:** *H**** **San Andrés** €10-40+ ✆ 948 648 472 + *Alb.* ❶ **Casa Mariela** *Priv.*[50÷5]* €7 ✆ 948 648 251. ❷ **la Pata & Oca** *Priv.[32÷3]*+ €10 ✆ 948 378 457. ❸ **Casa Mari** *Priv.*[26÷5]* €7 ✆ 948 648 409 c/Casas Nuevas. ❏ *Iglesia de Santo Sepulcro XII* (€1).
▐ **Viana:** *Turismo* ✆ 948 446 302. *Alb.* ❶ **Izar** *Priv.[18÷1]*+ €8-12 ✆ 948 090 002. ❷ **Santa Maria** *Par.[15÷4]* *€-donativo* ✆ 948 645 037. ❸ **Andrés Muñoz** *Mun.* *[54÷4]* €6 ✆ 948 645 530 c/San Pedro. *P*** **Casa Armendáriz** €30-40 c/ Navarro Villoslada 19. *P*** **San Pedro** €30-40 ✆ 948 645 927 c/Medio S.Pedro 13. *H**** **Palacio de Pujadas** €60-€80 ✆ 948 646 464 *cafetaria Portillo*. **Casa Asun** €25+ ✆ 948 645 149 c/La Rueda 46.

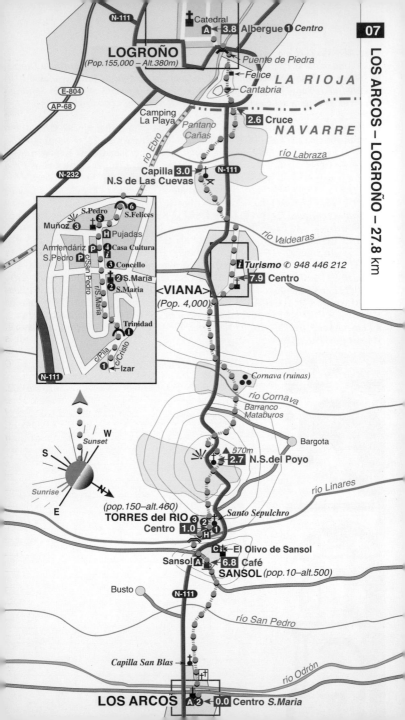

LOGROÑO: *Turismo:* c/Portales,50 © 941 291 260.
❑ *Monumentos:* ❶ *Puente de Piedra.* ❷ *Ermita San Gregorio y Casa de la Danza.*
❸ *Iglesia y claustro Santa Maria del Palacio XII.* ❹ *Iglesia San Bartolomé XIII.*
❺ *Catedral de Santa María de la Redonda XIV (Las Gemelas).* ❻ *Iglesia Santiago*
Real XVI. ❼ *Puerta del Camino Muralla del Revellín / Puerta Carlos.*

▌ *Albergues:* ❶ **Logroño** *Asoc.[68÷3]* €7 © 941 248 686 c/Ruaviejo, 32. ❷ **Santiago**
Apóstol *Priv.[68÷3]* €10 (+€30) © 941 256 976 c/Ruaviejo, 42. ❸ **Santiago** *Par.*
[30+÷3+] €-donativo c/Barricocepo, 8 adj. Iglesia de Santiago. ❹ **Logroño** *Priv.*
[30÷6]+ €10 (+€30) © 941 254 226 c/Capitán Gallarza, 10. ❺ **Entresueños** *Priv.*
[92÷10]+ €10 © 941 271 334 c/ Portales, 12 adj. catedral. ❻ **Check In Rioja** *Priv.*
[30÷1] €11-€15 © 941 272 329 c/Los Baños, 2. ❼ **Albas** *(Puerta del Revellín)*
Priv.*[22÷1] €11 © 941 700 832 Plaza Martínez Flamarique, 4 adj cafe *El Albero.*
▌ *Hostales:(entrada)* H*** **F&G** €60+ © 941 008 900 Av. Viana. P **Parque Del Ebro**
€15 © 616 840 786 Paseo de La Constitución 24. *(centro)* P* **Redondela** €30+ ©
941 272 409 c/Portales,21. P **Daniel** © 941 231 581 + P **Sebastian** © 665 974
651 + P **San Juan** © 941 231 581 c/San Juan. H*****Marqués de Vallejo** €50 © 941
248 333 c/Marqués de Vallejo,8. Hs** **La Numantina** © 941 251 411 Sagasta, 4. P
Villar © 941 220 228 plaza Matínez Zaporta adj. café Moderno. H*** **Mayor** €70+
© 941 232 368 c/Marqués. H*** **Portales** €80 © 941 502 794 c/ Portales, 85. *(salida)*
H*** **Murrieta** €50 © 941 224 150 Marqués de Murrieta, 1. P **Laurel** Gonzalo de
Berceo, 4. €37 © 941 225 154. P **El Camino** €27 © 618 65 50 00 c/ La Industria,2.
▌ *Planeta Agua 'trekking'* Av. de Navarra,8 © 941-252 764. *Lavanderia S.Mateo* c/
Doce,4 (08:00-22:00).

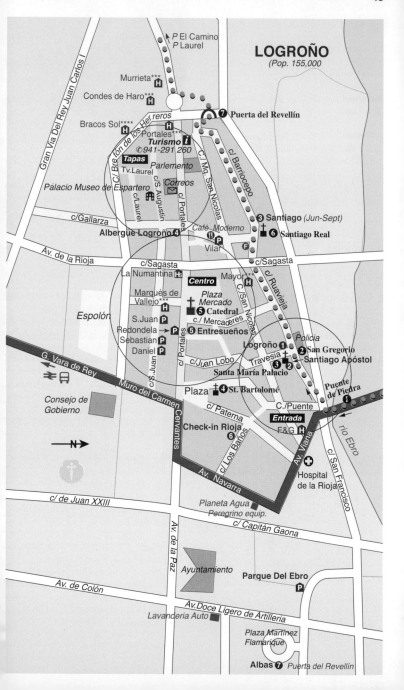

LOGROÑO
(Pop. 155,000)

P El Camino
P Laurel

Murrieta***
Condes de Haro***

Puerta del Revellín

Bracos Sol****
Portales***
Turismo
© 941-291 260
Tapas
Tv.Laurel
Parlemento

Palacio Museo de Espartero

c/Gallarza
Café_Moderno
Albergue Logroño
Vilar

Santiago *(Jun-Sept)*
Santiago Real

c/Sagasta
c/Sagasta

Av. de la Rioja

La Numantina
Centro
Mayor
Marqués de
Vallejo***
Plaza
Mercado
Catedral
Espolón
c./ Mercaderes
S.Juan
Redondela →
Entresueños
Sebastian
Logroño
San Gregorio
Daniel
Travesia
Santiago Apóstol
Santa María Palacio
Policia
G. Vara de Rey
Puente
de Piedra
Plaza
St. Bartolomé
Muro del Carmen
C./Puente
río Ebro
c/Paterna
Consejo de
Gobierno
Entrada
Check-in Rioja
F&G
c/Los Baños
N→
Av. Navarra
Hospital
de la Rioja

c/ de Juan XXIII
Planeta Agua
Peregrino equip.
c/ Capitán Gaona

Ayuntamiento
Parque Del Ebro

Av. de Colón
Av.Doce Ligero de Artilleria
Lavanderia Auto

Plaza Martínez
Flamarique

Albas Puerta del Revellín

08 **615.6** km (382.5 ml) – Santiago

LOGROÑO – NÁJERA (La Rioja)

⁓⁓⁓⁓	--- ---	23.1	--- ---	80%
━━━	--- ---	3.8	--- ---	13%
▬▬▬	--- ---	2.0	--- ---	7%
Total km		**28.9** km	(18.0 ml)	

◣◢ 30.4 km (+ 1.5 km)
Alto ▲ Poyo Roldán 600m (1,968 ft)
<**Ⓐ Ⓗ**> Navarrete **12.7** km – Ventosa **18.4** km *(opción + 1.4 km).*

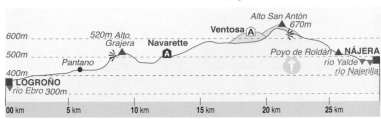

■ **Navarrete:** ● *Alb.* **El Camino de las Estrellas** *Priv.[40÷3]*+ €10 (+€40) ℭ 618 051 392. ❶ **La Casa del Peregrino** *Priv.[18÷1]*+ €8 (+€25) ℭ 630 982 928 *c/ Cruz.* ❷ **Navarrete Centro** *Asoc.[50÷4]* €7 ℭ 941 440 722 *adj. café Los Arcos.* ❸ **Buen Camino** *Priv.[6÷1]*+ €9 ℭ 941 440 318 *(Hs Villa c/ Cruz).* ❹ **Pilgrim's** *Priv. [32÷4]*+ €9 ℭ 941 441 550 c/Abadía. ❺ **El Cántaro** *Priv.[12÷1]*+ €10 (+€20) ℭ 941 441 180 c/Herrerías. ❻ **A la Sombra del Laurel** *Priv.[16÷2]*+ €15 +€30 ℭ 639 861 110 Carretera de Burgos, 52. ■ *Hostales:* Hs* **Villa de Navarrete** ℭ 941 440 318 c/La Cruz. H*** **Rey Sancho** ℭ 941 441 378 c/Mayor Alta + P* **Peregrinando** ℭ 941 441 324. H** **San Camilo** ℭ 941 441 111 N-120. ● ● ● ● *Sotés: (+1.5 km)* **alb. San Martín** *[8÷2]* €10 ℭ 650 962 625 c/ S.Miguel, 67. ● ● ● ● *Ventosa:* **alb. San Saturnino** *Priv.*[42÷6] €10 ℭ 941 441 899. H** **Las Águedas** €45-65 ℭ 941 441 774 Plaza S. Coloma. *AT* **Loft & Garden** €30+ ℭ 607 855 432.

■ **NÁJERA:** ❑ *Turismo* ℭ 941 360 041 Plaza San Miguel. ❑ ❶ *Conv. S. Elena.* ❷ *Puente.* ❸ *Monasterio S. María de la Real Pantheon Real.* ❹ *Castillo.*

■ *Alb.* ❶ **El Peregrino** *Priv.[20÷1]* €10 ℭ 941 896 027 c/ San Fernando 90. ❷ **Puerta de Nájera** *Priv.[34÷6]* €10-15 c/Carmen ℭ 941 362 317. ❸ **Calle Mayor** *Priv.[9÷1]*+ €9 + €50 c/ Dicarán,5 ℭ 941 360 407. ❹ **Nido de Cigüeña** *Priv.[19÷3]* €10-€15 + €35 ℭ 941 896 027 Calleja Cuarta San Miguel, 4. ❺ **Nájera** *Asoc.[90÷1]* €-donativo. ❻ **Sancho III** *Priv.[10÷2]* €10 ℭ 941 361 138 *La Judería* (menú €8). ❑ *Hostales:* Hs** **Ciudad de Nájera** €45+ ℭ 941 360 660 calleja San Miguel, 14. H*** **Duques de Nájera** €50+ ℭ 941 410 421 c/ Carmen, 7. Hs* **Hispano** €30 ℭ 941 363 615 c/La Cepa,2.

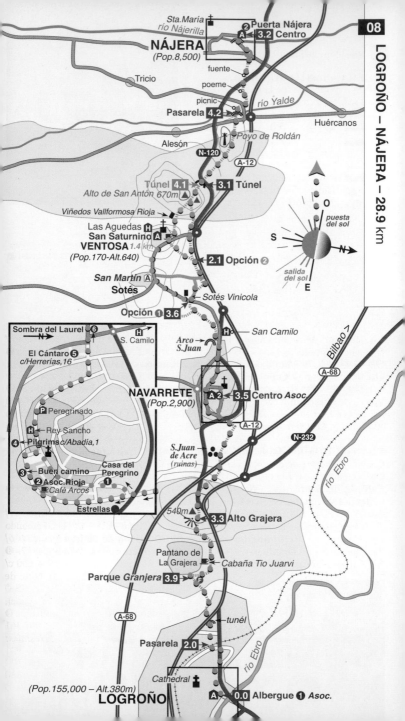

Sta.María
río Nájerilla
2 Puerta Nájera
3.2 Centro
NÁJERA
(Pop.8,500)
fuente
poeme
picnic
Pasarela **4.2**
río Yalde
Tricio
Huércanos
Alesón
Poyo de Roldán
N-120
A-12
Túnel **4.1**
Alto de San Antón 670m
3.1 Túnel
Viñedos Vallformosa Rioja
Las Aguedas
San Saturnino
VENTOSA *1.4 km*
(Pop.170-Alt.640)
2.1 Opción **2**
San Martín
Sotés
Sotés Vinicola
Opción **1** **3.6**

O
puesta del sol
S
N
salida del sol
E

H — San Camilo
Arco →
S.Juan
NAVARRETE
(Pop.2,900)
A 2 **3.5** Centro *Asoc*
A-12

Bilbao
A-68
N-232
río Ebro

S.Juan de Acre (ruinas)

540m **3.3** Alto Grajera

Pantano de La Grajera
Cabaña Tio Juarvi
Parque *Granjera* **3.9** →

A-68

tunél

Pasarela **2.0**

río Ebro

Cathedral
(Pop.155,000 – Alt.380m)
LOGROÑO
A **0.0** Albergue **1** *Asoc*.

Inset map (Navarrete):

Sombra del Laurel **6**
H S. Camilo
El Cántaro **5**
c/Herrerías,16
P Peregrinado
H — Rey Sancho
4 Pilgrims *c/Abadía,1*
3 — Buen camino
2 Asoc.Rioja
Café Arcos
Casa del Peregrino
1
Estrellas

09 **586.7** km (364.6 ml) – Santiago

NÁJERA – SANTO DOMINGO de la CALZADA

▓▓▓▓▓	--- ---	15.1	--- ---	71%
▬▬▬	--- ---	5.0	--- ---	23%
▬▬▬	--- ---	1.2	--- ---	6%
Total km		**21.3** km (13.2 ml)		

◣ --- --- 22.8 km (+ 1.5 km)
Alto ▲ Cirueña 745m (2,444 ft)
< A H > Azofra **6.1** km - Cirueña **15.5** km

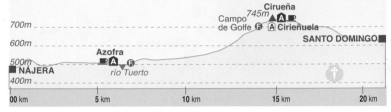

■ Azofra: *Alb.* ❶ **Azofra** *Muni.[60÷30]* €7 ☎ 941 379 220 c/Las Parras (+200m). ❷ **Herbert Simón** *Par.[26÷2]* ☎ 607 383 811 adj. *N.S. de los Ángeles. P* **La Plaza** €30-45 ☎ 941 379 239 Pl. de España 7. **Real Casona de las Amas** €80-160 ☎ 941 416 103 c/Mayor. ● *Cañas:* *Abadía Cisterciense de Cañas XII. Hs* **La Casona** ☎ 941-379 150 €24. *Hs* **La Posada del Santo** ☎ 941-204 187. **■ Cirueña:** *Alb.* ❶ **Virgen de Guadalupe** *Priv.*[23÷5]* €7 ☎ 638 924 069 c/ Barrio Alto. ❷ **Victoria** *Priv.*[12÷2]*+ €10-€30+ ☎ 941 426 105 c/S.Andres. *P** **Casa Victoria** €35+ ☎ 941 426 105 adj. *Café/bar Jacobeo.*

■ SANTO DOMINGO de la Calzada: *Turismo* ☎ 941 341 238 c/Mayor, 33 *Centro de Interpretación del Camino* (10:00–14:00 / 16:00–19:00). *Alb.* ❶ **Abadía Cistercienses** *Conv.[33÷5]* €5 ☎ 941 340 700 c/Mayor 29-31. ❷ **Casa de la Cofradía del Santo** *Asoc.[140÷4]* €7 ☎ 941 343 390. ❏ *Hostales: Hs**** **Hospedería Cistercienses** *(Santa Teresita)* €40+ ☎ 941 340 700 c/Pinar, 2. *H**** **El Corregidor** €40+ ☎ 941 342 128 c/Mayor,14. *Hs** **Rey Pedro I** €40 ☎ 941 341 160 c/S.Roque, 9. *Hs* **La Catedral** c/ Isidoro Salas 651 948 260. *P** **Miguel** €25+ ☎ 941 343 252 c/ Juan Carlos I, 23. *Hs** **El Molino de Floren** €40 ☎ 941 342 031 c/Margubete. *H***** **Parador de Santo Domingo** €90+ ☎ 941 340 300 Plaza del Santo (adj. catedral). *H**** **Parador Bernardo de Fresneda** €90+ ☎ 941 341 150.

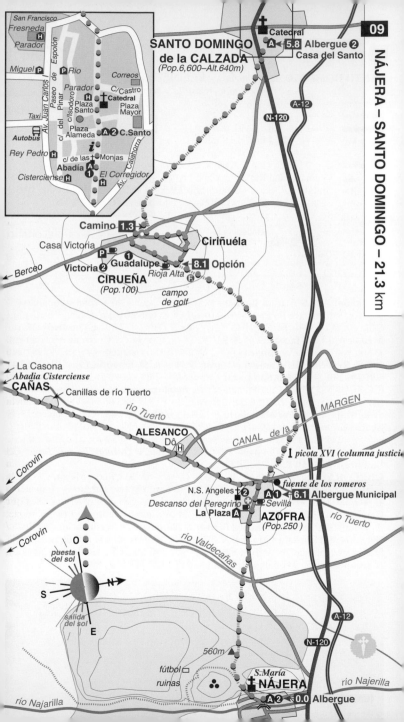

San Francisco
Fresneda
Parador

Miguel

C/ Castro
Correos

Paseo de Espolón
Rio
Parador
Plaza Santo
Catedral
Plaza Mayor

Taxi
C/ del Pinar
Av. Juan Carlos
C.Santo
Plaza Alameda

Autobus
Rey Pedro

Abadía
Cisterciense
C/ de las Monjas
El Corregidor
Av. Calatorra

SANTO DOMINGO
de la CALZADA
(Pop.6,600–Alt.640m)

Catedral
5.8 Albergue **2**
Casa del Santo

A-12
N-120

Camino **1.3**

Ciriñuéla

Casa Victoria
Guadalupe **8.1** Opción
Victoria **2**
CIRUEÑA
(Pop.100)
Rioja Alta
campo de golf

← Berceo

La Casona
Abadía Cisterciense
CAÑAS
Canillas de río Tuerto

río Tuerto
MARGEN

← Corovin

ALESANCO
Dô

CANAL de la

picota XVI (columna justici

← Corovin

puesta del sol

N.S. Angeles **2**
Descanso del Peregrino
La Plaza

fuente de los romeros
6.1 Albergue Municipal
Sevilla
1
AZOFRA
(Pop.250)
río Tuerto

S
E
salida del sol

río Valdecañas

560m ▲
fútbol
ruinas

S.María
NÁJERA
2 **0.0** Albergue

río Najerilla
río Najerilla

10 **565.4** km (351.3 ml) – Santiago

SANTO DOMINGO de la Calzada – BELORADO
La Rioja – Castilla y León

|||||||||||||||	--- ---	16.2	--- ---	72%
▬▬▬	--- ---	5.4	--- ---	24%
▬▬▬	--- ---	0.8		4%
Total km		**22.4** km	(13.9 ml)	

◣◢ --- --- 23.9 km (^300m + 1.5 km)

Alto ▲ Vilamayor del Río 810m (2,657 ft)

<🅰 🅷> Grañón **6.7** km – Carrasquedo **7.9** km (+1.2 km) – Redecilla **10.5** – Castildelgado **12.2** km (+200m) – Viloria de la Rioja **14.1** km.

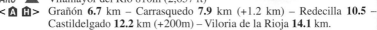

■ **Grañón:** *Alb.* ❶ S.Juan Bautista *Par.[40÷2]* €-donativo + cena comunitaria ℂ 941 420 818. ❷ **Ave de Paso** *Priv. [10÷2]* €6 ℂ 666 801 051 (Manu Pérez) c/ El Caño 19. ❸ **Casa de las Sonrisas** *Priv. [14÷2]* ℂ 687 877 891 €-donativo *c/Mayor Nº16*. @*Nº40 CR* **Jacobea** €45 ℂ 941 420 684. @*Nº34 CR* **Cerro de Mirabel** €50 ℂ 660 166 090. ● *Carrasquedo (+1.2 km): Alb.* **Carrasquedo** *[40]*+ €8 ℂ 941 746 000. ■ **Redecilla del Camino** *c/Mayor Nº34 Alb.* ❶ **Essentia** *Priv.[10÷2]* €7 ℂ 606 046 298. @*Nº24* ❷ San Lázaro *Muni.[40÷4]* €5 ℂ 686 563 548. *H* **Redecilla** €30 ℂ 947 585 256. ■ **Castildelgado:** *Alb.* **Bideluze** *Priv.[16÷2]*+ €10 +€30 ℂ 616 647 115 c/ Mayor, 8. *Hs* **El Chocalatero** €25+ ℂ 947 588 063 (+200m). ■ **Viloria de la Rioja** *Alb.* ❶ **Parada Viloria** *Priv.[16÷3]* €5 ℂ 639 451 660 c/Bajera, 37. ❷ **Acacio & Orietta** *Priv.[10÷1] V.* €5 ℂ 947 585 220 c/ Nueva. **MiHotelito** €70+ ℂ 947 585 225 Plaza Mayor, 16. ● *Villamayor del Río (+0.3 km): Alb.* **San Luis de Francia** *Priv.*[26÷8]* €5 / menú €8 ℂ 947 580 566. ● *Quintanilla del Monte: CR* **La Encantada** €50 ℂ 947 580 484.

■ **BELORADO:** *Turismo* (10:30-20:00) ℂ 941 341 238 Plaza Mayor. *Alb.* ❶ **A Santiago** *Priv.*[98÷8]* €5-7 ℂ 947 562 164. ❷ **Santa María** *Par.[24÷4]* €-donativo ℂ 947 580 085. ❸ **El Corro** *Muni.[40÷4]* €6 ℂ 947 581 419 c/ Mayor 68. ❹ **El Caminante** *Priv.*[22÷4]*+ €6 ℂ 947 580 231. ❺ **Cuatro Cantones** *Priv.[62÷5]* €7 ℂ 696 427 707 c/Hipólito Lopez Bernal. ❏ *Hostales: CR* **Verdeancho** ℂ 659 484 584 €50+. *CR* **Waslala** €25 – €45 ℂ 947 580 726 c/Mayor 57. *P* **Ojarre** P ℂ 947 580 223 c/Santiago 16. *P* **Toni** €30-40 ℂ 947 580 525 c/Redecilla del Campo 7. *H°***Jacobeo** €60 ℂ 947 580 010. *H* **Belorado** €25 ℂ 947 580 684.

La Rioja / Castilla y León

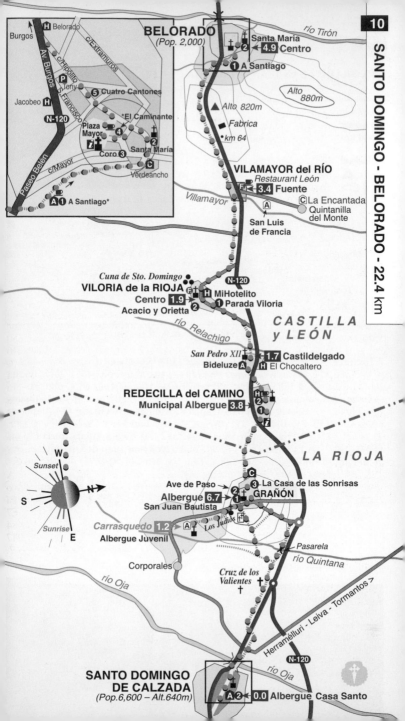

BELORADO
(Pop. 2,000)

Santa Maria **4.9** Centro

1 A Santiago

Burgos **H** Belorado

c/Extramuros

Av. Burgos

c/Hipólito

P Tony

H Jacobeo

5 Cuatro Cantones

N-120

c/ Francisco

El Caminante

Plaza Mayor

4

i Coro **3**

Santa María

C

Verdeancho

Paseo Belén

c/Mayor

A 1 A Santiago*

Alto 880m

▲ Alto 820m

■ *Fabrica*

• *km 64*

VILAMAYOR del RÍO

Restaurant León

F 3.4 Fuente

C La Encantada

A Quintanilla del Monte

Villamayor

A

San Luis de Francia

Cuna de Sto. Domingo ●

VILORIA de la RIOJA

Centro **1.9**

2

Acacio y Orietta

H MiHotelito

1 Parada Viloria

CASTILLA y LEÓN

río Relachigo

San Pedro XII

1.7 Castildelgado

Bideluze **A**

H El Chocaltero

REDECILLA del CAMINO

Municipal Albergue **3.8**

H

2

1

i

LA RIOJA

N

W

Sunset

S

Sunrise

E

Ave de Paso

2 **C**

3 La Casa de las Sonrisas

Albergue **6.7**

GRAÑÓN

San Juan Bautista

1

Carrasquedo **1.2**

A Los Judíos

Albergue Juvenil

■

Corporales ●

Cruz de los Valientes

†

Pasarela

río Quintana

Herramélluri - Leiva - Tormantos >

río Oja

SANTO DOMINGO DE CALZADA
(Pop.6,600 – Alt.640m)

N-120

río Oja

A 2 **0.0** Albergue Casa Santo

11 **543.0** km (337.4 ml) – Santiago

BELORADO – SAN JUAN de ORTEGA

⸱⸱⸱⸱⸱⸱⸱⸱⸱⸱⸱⸱	--- ---	22.5	--- ---	*93%*
▬▬▬	--- ---	1.5	--- ---	*6%*
▬▬▬	--- ---	0.2	--- ---	*1%*
Total km		**24.2** km	(15.0 ml)	

▲ --- --- 26.7 km (^500m + 2.5 km)
Alto ▲ Montes de Oca: 1,150m (3,773 ft)
< Ⓐ Ⓗ > Tosantos **4.8** km – Villambistia **6.8**
Epinosa del Camino **8.4** km – Villafranca **12.0** km. *[Agés 27.8 km]*

■ **Tosantos:** *Alb.*❶ **S. Francisco de Asís** *Par.[30÷3]* €-*donativo + cena comunitaria* ✆ 947 580 371. ❷ **Los Arancones** *Priv.[16÷1]* €10 ✆ 947 581 485 c/ de la Iglesia. *Bar El Castaño.* ■ **Villambistia:** *Alb.*San Roque *Muni.[14÷1]* €6 ✆ 680 501 887 (+200m). ■ **Espinosa del camino:** *Alb.*❶ *Priv.* ✆ 630 104 922. ❷ **La Campana** *Priv.[10÷2]* ✆ 678 479 361. ■ **Villafranca de Montes de Oca:** *Alb.* ❶ **Villafranca** *Mun.[60÷4]* €5-7 ✆ 691 801 211. ❷ **San Antón Abad** *Priv*.*[26÷2]*+ €5-10 +€60 ✆ 947 582 150 *Hs******San Antón Abad** ✆ 947 582 150. *CR* **La Alpargatería** €25+ ✆ 686 040 884. *Hs* **El Pajaro** €25+ ✆ 947 582 029. ■ **San Juan de Ortega:** *Alb.* **San Juan** *Par.[70÷3]* €7 ✆ 947 560 438. *CR* **La Henera** €40-50 ✆ 947 409 935 m: 606 198 734. *Iglesia de San Nicolás de Barri XV.*

Montes de Oca
Monumento de los Caídos

N-120

La Henera **C**

†**A** **8.6** ← **Albergue San Juan**
San JUAN de ORTEGA
(Pop. 20 – Alt. 950m)

Ermita Valdefuente †**F**

Puerto Pedraja 1,095m

▲ *Alto 1,120m*

W
Sunset
N
S
Sunrise
E

arroyo Peroja

m **3.6** **Monumento** *a los Caídos*
▲

F **Fuente de Mojapán**

Virgen de Oca
F *Pozo S.Indalecio*
† *N.S.de Alba*

2 **San Antón Abad**
H San Antón Abad ***
VILLAFRANCA MONTES DE OCA
Municipal Albergue **3.6** **1** *(Pop. 200 – Alt. 950m)*
P El Pajaro

Embalse de Alba

rio Oca
rio Oca

San Felices
(ruinas)

2 **La Campana**
1 **1.6** **ESPINOSA del CAMINO**
Epinosa

VILLAMBISTIA
Iglesia *San Roque* **2.0** → **A** **San Roque**

Ermita Virgen de la Peña †

TOSANTOS
San Francisco de Asís Albergue **4.8** **1**
2 **Los Arancones**

N-120

San Miguel de Podroso

río Tirón

BELORADO
(Pop. 2,000 – Alt. 770m)
† *Santa María*
† **A** **2** ← **0.0** **Albergue**

12 **518.8** km (322.4 ml) – Santiago

SAN JUAN de ORTEGA – BURGOS

▦▦▦▦▦▦▦	--- ---	17.7 --- ---	68%
▬▬▬▬	--- ---	4.4 --- ---	17%
▬▬▬	--- ---	<u>4.0</u> --- ---	15%
Total km		**26.1** km	(16.2 ml)

◣◣◣ --- --- 27.1 km (^200m + 1.0 km)
Alto ▲ Sierra Atapuerca 1,080m (3,543 ft)
<**A H**> Agés **3.6** km – Atapuerca **6.1** km – Olmos de Atapuerca alt. **8.5** km.
Cardeñuela **12.4** km – Orbaneja **14.5** km – Castañares **19.1** km.

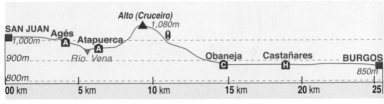

■ **Agés:** Alb. ❶ **San Rafael** Priv.[34÷6]+ €10 ✆ 947 430 392 menú. ❷ **Casa Caracol** Priv.[9÷2] ✆ 947 430 413. ❸ **El Pajar** Priv.*[32÷4] €9 ✆ 947 400 629 menú. **La Casa Roja.** ❹ **Agés** Muni.[36÷1] €8-10 + Bar La Taverna menú. ■ *Santovenia De Oca / N-120 (+3.9 km)* H** *Sierra de Atapuerca* €40 ✆ 947 106 912 ■ **Atapuerca:** Alb. ❶ **El Peregrino** Priv.*[36÷6]+ €8+€35 ✆ 661 580 882. ❷ **La Hutte** Priv. [18÷1] €5 ✆ 947 430 320 (+300m). CR **Papasol** €50. CR **El Palomar** €20-40 incl. ✆ 947 430 549 + Rest. terraza c/ Revilla 22. ● *Olmos de Atapuerca: (+2.4 km)* Alb. **Olmos** La Golondrina Muni.[21÷3] €7 ✆ 661 026 495 + Meson los Hidalgos menú. ■ **Cardeñuela Riopico:** Alb. ❶ **Vía Minera** Priv.[20÷4]+ €8 +€40 c/ La Iglesia ✆ 652 941 647 (+200m) menú. ❷ **Cardeñuela** Muni.[16÷1] €5 ✆ 646 249 597 + Bar La Parada. ❸ **Santa Fe** Priv. [10÷1]+ €8 +€35 Miryam ✆ 947 560 722 m: 626 352 269 menú. CR **La Cardeñuela** €50 ✆ 947 210 479. ■ **Orbaneja** Calle Principal Alb. **Orbaneja** Muni.[18÷1]+ €5 ✆ 648 604 577. Bar El Peregrino. CR **Fortaleza** €50 ✆ 678 116 570.
❶● **Castañares N-120:** H*** **Versus** €45 ✆ 947 474 977.
❷● **Villafría**: H**Buenos Aires** €25 ✆ 947 483 770. Hs**Iruñako** €30 ✆ 947 484 126
❸● **Parque Fluvial**: Camping **Fuente Blancas** hostel €9 ✆ 947 486 016.

❸● Parque Fluvial

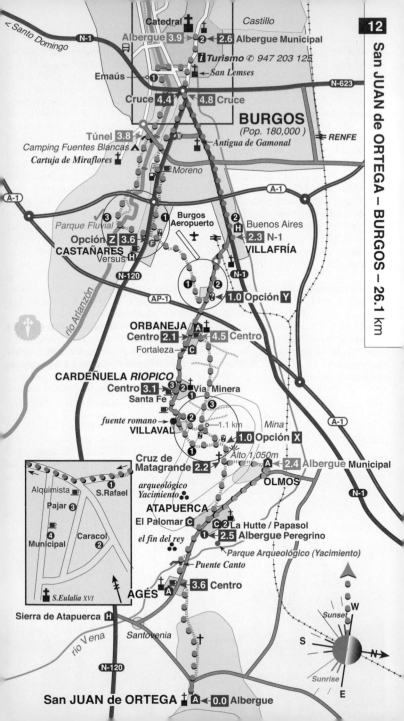

Santo Domingo

N-1

Catedral ✝

Castillo

Albergue **3.9** → **2** ← **2.6** Albergue Municipal

🚌

i *Turismo* ☏ 947 203 125

Emaús

1

← San Lemses

Cruce **4.4** ← **4.8** Cruce

N-623

BURGOS
(Pop. 180,000)

→ *RENFE*

Túnel **3.8**

Camping Fuentes Blancas ⋀

Cartuja de Miraflores ✝

✝ *Antigua de Gamonal*

Moreno

A-1

Parque Fluvial

3

1

Burgos
Aeropuerto

2
H

Buenos Aires

2.3 N-1

Opción **Z** **3.6**

CASTAÑARES

Versus **H**

F

VILLAFRÍA

N-1

N-120

AP-1

1

2

1.0 Opción **Y**

ORBANEJA

Centro **2.1** → **A** ✝

4.5 Centro

Fortaleza

C

CARDEÑUELA *RIOPICO*

Centro **3.1** **3** **2** ← Vía Minera

Santa Fe

1

3

fuente romano →

2

Mina

VILLAVAL

1.1 km

1

1.0 Opción **X**

Cruz de
Matagrande **2.2**

✝ Alto *1,050m*

A **2.4** Albergue Municipal

arqueológico
Yacimiento ⚫⚫⚫

OLMOS

N-1

ATAPUERCA

El Palomar **C**

C **2** La Hutte / Papasol

1 **2.5** Albergue Peregrino

el fin del rey

Parque Arqueológico (Yacimiento)

✝ *Puente Canto*

✝ **A** → **3.6** Centro

AGÉS

Santovenia

Sierra de Atapuerca **H**

río Vena

N-120

✝

San JUAN de ORTEGA ✝ **A** ← **0.0** Albergue

Alquimista **1** **1** S.Rafael

Pajar **3**

☕

4
Municipal

Caracol **2**

✝ S.Eulalia *XVI*

W
Sunset

S

N

Sunrise

E

BURGOS: ❏ *Turismo* Plaza Alonso,7 ✆ 947 203 125. ▮ *Albergues:* ❶ **Casa de Peregrinos Emaús** *Par.[20÷4]* C/ de San Pedro de Cardeña. ❷ **La Casa del Cubo** *Lerma Asoc.[150÷6]* €5 ✆ 947 460 922. ❸ **Divina Pastora** *Asoc.[16÷1]* €5 ✆ 947 207 952 c/Laín Calvo, 10. ❹ **Hostel Burgos** *Priv.[120]*+ €18 +€30-40 ✆ 947 250 801 c/ Miranda, 4 (estación de autobuses). ▮ *Hostales Centro:* €25-55**:** *Plaza S. Lemses* (c/Cardenal Benlloch) *Hsr** **Acacia** ✆ 947 205 134. *Hs** **Monjes Magnos** ✆ 947 205 134. *Hs** **Lar** €25 ✆ 947 209 655. *Hsr** **Carrales** ✆ ✆ 947 263 547 c/ Puente Gasset 4. *Hsr** **Manjón** ✆ 947 208 689 c/Gran Teatro adj. *H**** **Almirante Bonifaz** ✆ 947 206 943. *Barrio antigua: H*** **La Puebla** ✆ 947 203 350 c/La Puebla N°4 + N°6 *Hr*** **Cordón** ✆ 947 265 000. *Hr* **El Jacobeo** ✆ 947 260 102 c/ San Juan *Hr*** **Centro Los Braseros** ✆ 947 252 958. *Hsr** **Norte y Londres** ✆ 947 264 125. *Plazas Libertad & Mayor*: *Hr* **García** ✆ 947 205 553 c/Santander, 1. *Hsr* **Hidalgo** ✆ 947 203 481 c/Almirante Bonifaz, 14. *H** **España** ✆ 947 206 340 Paseo Espolón. *c/Fernán González* €65+**:** *H**** **Palacio de los Blasones** ✆ 947 271 000 @ N°10. *H**** **Mesón del Cid II** ✆ 947 208 715 @N°62. *H**** **Abba Burgos** ✆ 947 001 100 @ N°72. *Hr** **Conde de Miranda** ✆ 947-265 267 c/Miranda, 4 (adj. estación de autobuses). *H*** **Via Gotica** ✆ 947 244 444 Plaza de Vega. *H**** **NH Palacio de la Merced** €75+ ✆ 947 479 900 c/Merced.

❏ **Monumentos históricos:** ❶ *San Lesmes XIV & Mo. S. Juan (mueso Marceliano)* ❷ *Arco S. Juan XIII* ❸ *Casa del Cordón XV* ❹ *San Gil XIV* ❺ *S. Esteban XIV (mueso Retablo)* ❻ *S. Nicolas de Barri XV* ❼ *Catedral de Santa María XIII* (9:30-18:30) €7 (+ credencial €3.50). ❽ *Arco & Puente de Santa María XIV* ❾ *Solar del Cid* ❿ *Arco S.Martin XIII.* ●-11 *Santa María la Real de Las Huelgas XII (museo).* ●-12 *Hospital del Rey XII (antiguo hospital del peregrino).* ● *Cartuja de Miraflores XV (+4 km).* ● *Museo de la Evolución de Humana* Paseo Sierra de Atapuerca (10:00-14:30 / 16:30-20:00) €6.

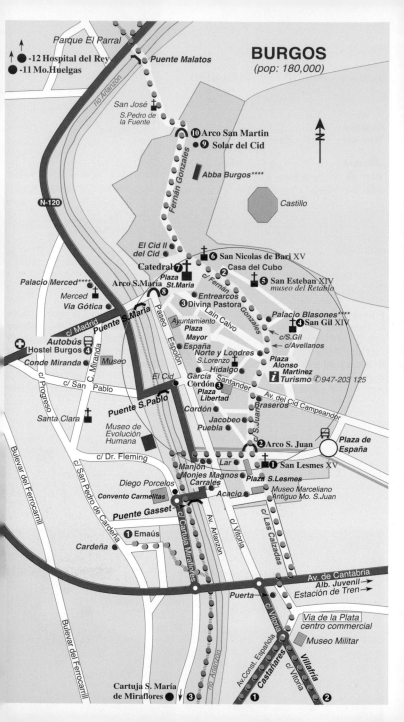

13 **492.7** km (306.2 ml) – Santiago

BURGOS – HORNILLOS del CAMINO

▓▓▓▓▓▓	--- ---	14.0	--- ---	67%
	--- ---	3.2	--- ---	15%
▬▬▬	--- ---	<u>3.8</u>	--- ---	18%
Total km		**21.0** km	(13.0 ml)	

21.7 km (^150m + 0.7 km)
Alto ▲ Meseta 950m (3,117 ft)
< 🄰 🄷 > N-120 Burgos **2.2** km – Tarjados **10.6** – Rabé de las Calzadas **13.0** km.

Alto *(Meseta)*
950m ▲
900m
■ **BURGOS**
800m
Tarjados 🄰 **Rabé** 🄰
Río Arlanzón
HORNILLOS
825m
00 km   5 km   10 km   15 km   20 km

▮ **Burgos N-620 and N-120:** *H*[**] **Puerta Romeros** ✆ 947 460 738. *Hs*[***]**Abadía Camino Santiago** ✆ 947 040 404 and *Hs*[**]**Via Láctea** ✆ 947 463 211. ▮ **Tardajos:** *Alb.* ❶ **La Fábrica** *Priv.[14÷4]*+ €12 +€35 ✆ 646 000 908 c/La Fábrica + *menú.* ❷ **La Casa de Beli** *Priv.[30÷3]*+ €10-€45+ ✆ 947 451 234 ❸ **Tardajos** *Muni.[18÷3]* €-*donativo* ✆ 947 451 189 adj. *Bar El Camino.* P **Mary** €15-20 ✆ 947 451 125 c/ Pozas N-120. ▮ **Rabé de las Calzadas:** *H*[**] **Deobrigula** €35 60 ✆ 947 560 540 c/ Alta. *Alb.* ❶ **Libéranos Dómine** *Priv.[24÷4]* €8 ✆ 695 116 901 + *menú* €8 + *Bar La Peña.* ❷ **Ospital Santa Marina y Santiago** *Priv.[8÷1]* €8 *(Michelle y Félix)* ✆ 670 971 919 *menú donativo.* ▮ **Hornillos del Camino:** *Alb.* ❶ **El Alfar** *Priv.[20÷3]* €9 *Pilar* ✆ 619 235 930 + *menú* € 8. ❷ **Meeting Point** *Priv.[32÷3]* €9 *Omar* ✆ 608 113 599. ❸ **Hornillos** *Muni.[32÷3]* €5 ✆ 689 784 681. *Casa Manolo* ✆ 947 411 050 *menú.* *CR* **de sol a sol** €35 ✆ 649 876 091. *CR* **La Casa del Abuelo** €30+ ✆ 661 869 618.

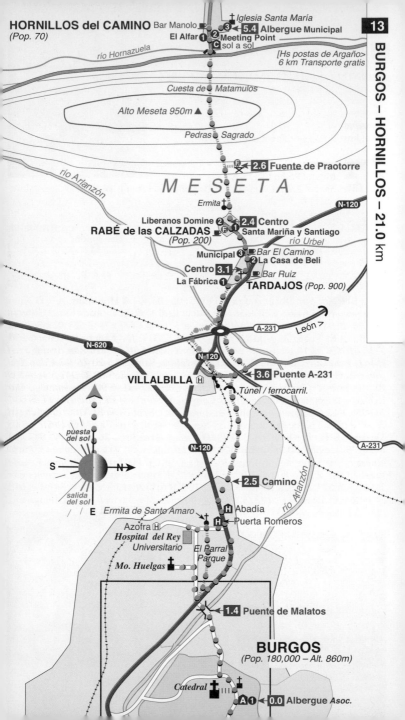

HORNILLOS del CAMINO Bar Manolo
(Pop. 70)
† *Iglesia Santa María*
❸ **5.4 Albergue Municipal**
❷ **Meeting Point**
El Alfar ❶
C **sol a sol**

río Hornazuela

[Hs postas de Argaño> 6 km Transporte gratis]

Cuesta de Matamulos

Alto Meseta 950m ▲

Pedras Sagrado

P **2.6 Fuente de Praotorre**

M E S E T A

río Arlanzón

† *Ermita*

Liberanos Domine ❷ **2.4 Centro**
RABÉ de las CALZADAS ❶ Santa Mariña y Santiago
(Pop. 200)
río Urbel

Municipal ❸ *Bar El Camino*
❷ *La Casa de Beli*
Centro **3.1** † *Bar Ruiz*
La Fábrica ❶ **TARDAJOS** *(Pop. 900)*

A-231 León >

N-620

N 120

◄ 3.6 Puente A-231

VILLALBILLA Ⓗ

† *Túnel / ferrocarril.*

A-231

N-120

◄ 2.5 Camino

río Arlanzón

puesta del sol

S ◄───► N

salida del sol

E

Ⓗ **Abadía**
Ermita de Santo Amaro †
Ⓗ **Puerta Romeros**
Azofra Ⓗ
Hospital del Rey Universitario †
El Parral Parque
Mo. Huelgas

◄ 1.4 Puente de Malatos

BURGOS
(Pop. 180,000 – Alt. 860m)

Catedral ††
Ⓐ❶ **◄ 0.0 Albergue** *Asoc.*

13

14 **471.7** km (293.1 ml) – Santiago

HORNILLOS del CAMINO – CASTROJERIZ

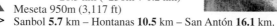

⊥⊥⊥⊥⊥⊥⊥⊥⊥	--- ---	13.7 --- ---	68%
	--- ---	6.4 --- ---	32%
▬▬▬	--- ---	0.0	
Total km	--- ---	**20.1** km (12.5 ml)	

◣ --- --- 21.3 km (^250m + 1.2 km)
Alto ▲ Meseta 950m (3,117 ft)
< Ⓐ Ⓗ > Sanbol **5.7** km – Hontanas **10.5** km – San Antón **16.1** km.

Elevation profile:
900m / Alto Meseta / San Bol / Alto (Meseta) 940m
HORNILLOS / Río Sanbol / 800m / Hontanas / Arco San Antón / CASTROJERIZ 800m
700m
00 km — 5 km — 10 km — 15 km — 20

▌ **San Bol:** *Alb.* **San Bol** *Muni.[12÷1]* €5 ℘ 606 893 407. ▌ **Hontanas:** *Alb.* ❶ **Juan de Yepes** *Priv.[54÷9]*+ €7 ℘ 638 938 546 c/ Real 1. ❷ **El Puntido** *Priv.*[50÷4]*+ €5–€25 ℘ 947 378 597. ❸ **Santa Brígida** *Priv.*[16÷3]* €7 ℘ 628 927 317. ❹ **San Juan** *El Nuevo* *Muni.[55÷2]* €5 ℘ 628 927 317. *Hs** **Fuente Estrella** ℘ 947 377 261. *CR* **El Descanso** ℘ 947 377 035. ▌ **San Antón:** *Alb.* **San Antón** *Priv. [14÷1]* €-donativo. ▌ **CASTROJERIZ:** ❶ *Iglesia Santa María N.S Manzano XIV y museo.* ❷ *Iglesia de Santo Domingo y museo.* ❸ *Iglesia San Juan y museo.Hs** **El Manzano** ℘ 620 782 768. *Alb.* ❶ **Orion** *Priv.[22÷3]*+ €11+€30-50 menú €10 *V.* ℘ 649 481 609 c/ Colegiata 28. ❷ **Camino de Santiago** *Priv.[32÷1]*+ €6 ℘ 947 377 255 + **El Camping** + *CR* **del Camping** €30. *c/Real Oriente: Hs*** **La Cachava** ℘ 947 378 547 Nº83. ❸ **Ultriea** *Priv.[40÷2]*+ €9+€40 ℘ 947 378 640 Nº77. *CR* **El Veredero** €30+ ℘ 696 985 323 Nº72. ❹ **Casa Nostra** *Priv.[26÷3]* ℘ 947 377 493 Nº54 *CR* **Grevillea** ℘ 947 378 644 Nº36. *Hs* **La Taberna** ℘ 947 377 120 Nº43. *Plaza Mayor alb.* ❺ **San Esteban** *Muni.[30÷1]* €5 ℘ 947 377 001 (*Casa Cultura*). *Posada* **Emebed** €45 ℘ 616 802 473 Plaza Mayor, 5. *H*****Puerta del Monte** *Iacobus* €35 ℘ 947 378 647. *H**** **La Posada** €45 ℘ 947 378 610. *H*** **El Mesón** ℘ 947 378 610 c/Cordón. ❻ **Rosalía** *Priv.[32÷5]* €10 ℘ 947 373 714 (Javier). ❼ **San Juan** *Asoc. [28÷2]* €-donativo ℘ 947 377 400.

CASTROJERIZ
(pop. 500)

San Esteban
A **1.5** Albergue **5**

Castillo (ruins)

2.5

½ km
Convento de Sta. Clara

Convento (ruins)
SAN ANTÓN
Arco de San Antón
A
San Antón
5.6 Arco

San Miguel (ruins)

CASTROJERIZ (inset map)

Museo
San Juan ↗ *S. Juan* **3**
Rosalía **5** S. Esteban
Mesón **H** **6** Plaza *Concello*
7 Mayor **H** Ermedd
Posada **H**
Puerta del Monte **H**
Museo **H**
Palacio (ruins) **F** **H** La Taberná
Veredero **C** † *Museo*
Casa Nostra **4** **2** S.Domingo
Monasterio (ruins) **3** Ultreia
H La Cachava
El Camping **2**
< Sta. Clara ½ km
Orion **1**
El Manzano **H**
† **1**
Colegiáta de La Virgen del Manzano

Castillo (ruins)

2.0 km

(Pop. 70) **HONTANAS** **4** ← Hontanos *muni.*
3
Centro **4.8** ■ Santa Brígida
Fuente Estrella **C** **2** El Puntido
Juan de Yepes **1**
Alto 950m
Castellanos de Castro

Villandiego

Iglesias

SAN BOL
San Bol *muni.* **A**
5.7 Cruce *San Bol*
río San Bol

Sunset **W**
S
N
Sunrise
E

M E S E T A

HORNILLOS del CAMINO
(Pop. 60– Alt. 820m)
Manolo ← **0.0** Centro

15 **451.6** km (280.6 ml) – Santiago

CASTROJERIZ – FRÓMISTA
(Burgos) (Palencia)

▓▓▓▓▓▓	--- ---	22.0	--- --- 88%
▬▬▬▬	--- ---	2.9	--- --- 12%
▬▬▬▬	--- ---	0.0	
Total km	--- ---	**24.9** km	(15.5 ml)

▲▲ --- --- 26.1 km (+ 1.2 km)
Alto ▲ Alto Mostelares 900m (2,952 ft)
< Ⓐ Ⓗ > Puente de Itero (S.Nicolas) **8.9** km – *Itero del Castillo 8.9 (+1.4 km)* – Itero de la Vega **10.6** km – Boadilla **19.1** km.

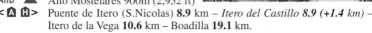

●●●● *Itero del Castillo (+1.5 km)*. Alb. Mun.*[12÷1]* €10 ✆ 642 213 560 (Toni) c/ Sol. ▮ **San Nicolás:** Alb. San Nicolás Asoc.*[12÷1]* €-donativo. ▮ **Itero de la Vega:** Hs + Alb. ❶ **Puente Fitero** Priv.*[22÷2]*+ €8 +€30-40 ✆ 979 151 822 c/ Santa María (entrada). Alb. ❷ **La Mochila** Priv.*[22÷3]* €6-10 Menú ✆ 979 151 781 c/Santa Ana. ❸ **Hogar del Peregrino** Priv.*[8÷4]* €12 + Menú ✆ 970 151 866 c/Santa Maria. ❹ **Muni.***[12÷1]* €5 ✆ 605 034 347 adj. *iglesia San Pedro XVI* Plaza Iglesia. ▮ **Boadilla del Camino:** Alb. ❶ **Putzu** Priv.*[16÷5]* €7. ❷ **Escuela** Muni.*[12÷1]* ✆ 979 810 390 €3 c/Escuelas. ❸ **En El Camino** Priv.***[48÷2]* €7 ✆ 979 810 284 m:619 105 168 + H* **Rural en el Camino** €35. ❹ **Titas** Priv.*[10÷1]* €10 ✆ 979 810 776.

▮ **FRÓMISTA** (pop. 840): Alb. ❶ **Canal de Castilla** Priv.*[16÷1]*+ €17 +€20-30 incl. menú ✆ 979 810 193 adj. estación de tren. ❷ **Frómista** Muni.*[56÷6]* €8 ✆ 979 811 089 m: 686 579 702 (Carmen) Plaza San Martín. HR* **San Martín** €40-50 ✆ 979 810 000. P **Marisa** ✆ 979 810 023. CR **Antonio y Marcelino y Serviarias** ✆ 626 959 079. Av. del Ejército Español *(c/Mayor):* Hs* **San Pedro** €35-45 ✆ 979 810 409. Hs* **El Apóstol** €37+ ✆ 979 810 255. Hs* **Camino de Santiago** €25-50 ✆ 979 810 282 +adj. ❸ **Estrella del Camino** Priv.*[34÷3]* €9. ❹ **Betania** Priv.*[5÷3]* ✆ 638 846 043 €-donativo (winter/invierno). H*** **Doña Mayor** €60+ ✆ 979 810 588 c/ Francesa 31. P **La Vía Láctea** €32+ ✆ 696 009 803 c/ Julio Senador 2. ❏ *Monumentos históricos:* ❶ *Iglesia de San Martín XI.* ❷ *Iglesia de San Pedro XV.* ❸ *Iglesia Santa María del Castillo (Leyenda del Camino).*

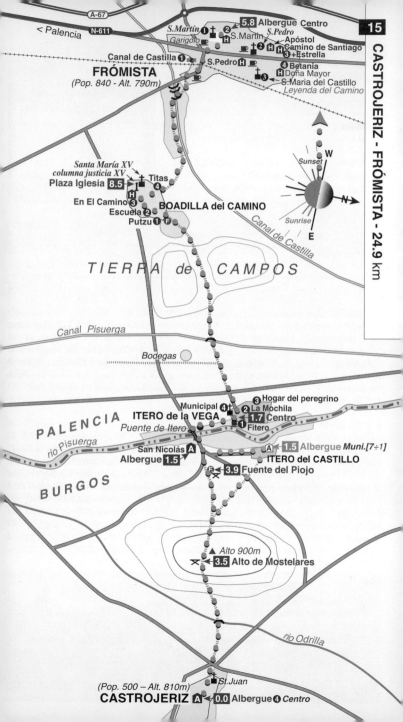

16 **426.7** km (265.1 ml) – Santiago

FRÓMISTA – CARRIÓN DE LOS CONDES

ⅰⅰⅰⅰⅰⅰⅰⅰⅰⅰⅰ	--- ---	16.1 --- ---	83%
▬▬▬▬	--- ---	3.2 --- ---	17%
▬▬▬	--- ---	0.0	
Total km	--- ---	**19.3** km (12.0 ml)	

▲ --- --- 19.5 km (^50m + 0.2 km)
Alto ▲ Carrión 830m (2,725 ft)
<Ⓐ Ⓗ> Población **3.4** km – Villarmentero **9.3**
Villalcázar de Sirga **13.6** km.

■ **Población de Campos:** *Alb.* **La Finca** *Priv.[20÷2]* €9 ℭ 979 067 028. *Alb.* **Escuela** *Muni.[18÷1]* €4 adj. *Hs*ˣ**Amanecer** ℭ 979 811 099 €30 + *menú* €9. ■ **Villarmentero de Campos:** *Alb.* **Amanecer** *Priv.[18÷2]* €6 + tipi €3! ℭ 629 178 543 *menú* €8. *CR* **Casona de Doña Petra** €35 ℭ 979 065 978. ■ **Villalcázar de Sirga** *Alb.*❶ **Villalcázar** *Muni.[20÷2]* €-*donativo* ℭ 979 888 041 Plaza del Peregrino. ❷ **Tasca Don Camino** *Priv.[28÷4]*+ €7-15 ℭ 979 888 053 + *CR* **Aurea.** *HsR*ˣ **Infanta Doña Leonor** €35 ℭ 927 888 015 Plaza Mayor. *CR* **Las Cántigas** €30 ℭ 979 888 027. *Iglesia Santa María la Virgen Blanca XIII.*

■ **CARRION DE LOS CONDES:** *Turismo* ℭ 979 880 932. *Monumentos:* ❶ *Museo y Real Monasterio y Ermita de La Piedad XIII.* ❷ *Iglesia de Santa María del Camino XII.* ❸ *Iglesia de Santiago XII museo* €1. ■ *Albergues:* ❶ **Santa Clara** *Conv.[30÷6]*+ €5–€22 ℭ 979 880 837 *Madres Clarisas.* ❷ **Santa María** *Par.[52÷3]* €5 ℭ 979 880 768. ❸ **Espíritu Santo** *Conv.[90÷7]* €5 *Hijas de San Vicente de Paul* ℭ 979 880 052 Plaza San Juan. ❹ **Casa de espiritualidad N.S de Belén** *Conv. [52÷52!+40÷20]* €22 (€28 incl.) ℭ 979 880 031 *R.R Filipenses.* ❏ *Hostales:* **Hs**ˣ **La Corte** €45 ℭ 979 880 138 c/Santa María, 34. *HsR*ˣ **Santiago** €35 ℭ 979 881 052 Plaza de los Regentes. *CR* **La Abuela Me** adj' *café Yadira* Plaza Conde Garay. *P*ˣ **El Resbalon** ℭ 979 880 433 c/Fernan Gomez, 19. *Hs* **Albe** €35 ℭ 699 094 185 Esteban Colantes,2. *H*ˣˣˣ **Real Monasterio San Zoilo** €60+ ℭ 979 880 050.

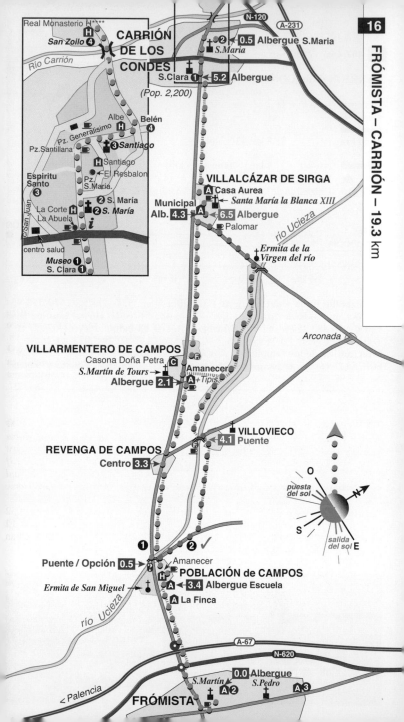

N-120 **A-231**

Real Monasterio H★★★★

H 2 **0.5** Albergue S.Maria
San Zoilo **H** 4
CARRIÓN ⊠ *S.Maria*
DE LOS
CONDES ✝
S. Clara 1 ◄ **5.2** Albergue

(Pop. 2,200)

Albe
H 4 Belén
Pz. Generalísimo

Pz.Santillana ✝ 3 *Santiago*

VILLALCÁZAR DE SIRGA
A Casa Aurea
✝ *Santa María la Blanca XIII*

H Santiago
←El Resbalon
Pz.
S.María

Municipal
Alb. **4.3** A ◄ **6.5** Albergue
□ Palomar

Espíritu
Santo
3

2 S. María
2 *S. María*

✝ *Ermita de la*
Virgen del río

La Corte **H**
La Abuela *i*

rio Ucieza

San Juan

centro salud

Museo 1
S. Clara 1

Arconada

VILLARMENTERO DE CAMPOS
F
Casona Doña Petra C
S.Martín de Tours → ■ **Amanecer**
Albergue **2.1** A ✝ *Tipis.*

VILLOVIECO
F ◄ **4.1**
Puente

REVENGA DE CAMPOS
F
Centro **3.3**

O
puesta
del sol

S

salida
del sol E

1 2 ✓

Puente / Opción **0.5** ← *Amanecer*
H ■ **POBLACIÓN de CAMPOS**
Ermita de San Miguel → ✝ A **3.4** Albergue Escuela
A La Finca

río Ucieza

A-67
N-620

0.0 Albergue
S.Martín ✝ A 2 *S.Pedro* ■ A 3

< *Palencia*

FRÓMISTA

17 407.4 km (253.2 ml) – Santiago

CARRIÓN de los CONDES – TERRADILLOS
de los TEMPLARIOS

....	--- ---	18.7	--- ---	70%
▬▬▬	--- ---	8.1	--- ---	30%
	--- ---	0.0		
Total km		**26.8** km (16.7 ml)		

▲▲▲ --- --- 27.3 km (^100m + 0.5 km)

Alto ▲ Ledigos alto 900m (2,950 ft)

< 🅰 🅷 > Calzadilla de la Cueza **17.3** km – Ledigos **23.4** km.

900m — **Calzada Romana** ------- **Calzadilla** **910m** **TERRADILLOS Ledigos**
CARRIÓN **Río Cueza** **880m**
800m *Río Carrión*

| 00 km | 5 km | 10 km | 15 km | 20 km | 25 km |

▮ **Calzadilla de la Cueza:** *Alb.* ❶ **Calzadilla** *Muni.*[34÷2] €5 ℰ 670 558 954 adj. ❷ **Camino Real** *Priv.*[80÷2] €7 ℰ 616 483 517 + *Hs* **Hostal Camino Real** €30 ℰ 979 883 187 *menú* €10. ▮ **Ledigos:** *Alb.* ❶ **El Palomar** *Priv.*[52÷7] €6-8 ℰ 979 883 614. ❷ **La Morena** *Priv.*[37÷8] €8-€15 ℰ 979 065 052 c/ Carretera 3. ▮ **Terradillos de los Templarios:** *Alb.* ❶ **Los Templarios** *Priv.*[34÷6]+ €7+€28 ℰ 667 252 279 *menú*. ❷ **Jacques de Molay** *Priv.*[49÷9] €8-10 ℰ 979-883 679 *menú*.

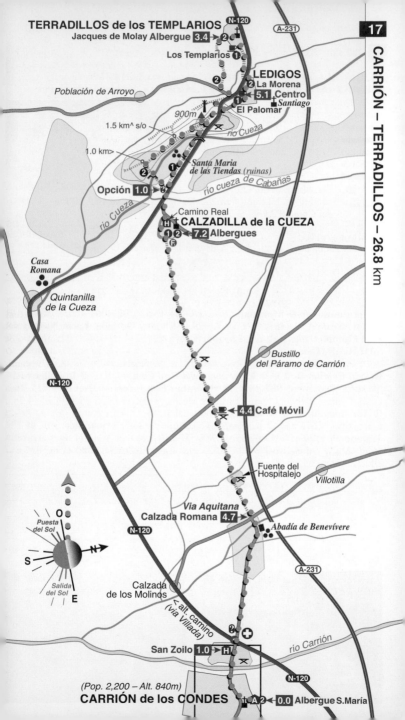

TERRADILLOS de los TEMPLARIOS
Jacques de Molay Albergue **3.4** → **2**
Los Templarios **1**

N-120
A-231

LEDIGOS
2 La Morena
5.1 ← Centro
Santiago
El Palomar

Población de Arroyo

900m
1.5 km^ s/o
1.0 km>

*Santa María
de las Tiendas* (ruinas)
río Cueza
río cueza de Cabañas
Opción **1.0** → **2**
río Cueza

Camino Real
H **CALZADILLA de la CUEZA**
1 **2** ← **7.2** Albergues
F

*Casa
Romana*

*Quintanilla
de la Cueza*

*Bustillo
del Páramo de Carrión*

4.4 ← Café Móvil

N-120

Fuente del
Hospitalejo
Villotilla

Vía Aquitana
Calzada Romana **4.7** →
Abadía de Benevívere

A-231

*Calzada
de los Molinos*
< alt. camino
(vía Vilada)

río Carrión

San Zoilo **1.0** → **H**

N-120

(Pop. 2,200 – Alt. 840m)
CARRIÓN de los CONDES
A 2 ← **0.0** Albergue S.María

O
*Puesta
del Sol*
S — N
*Salida
del Sol*
E

18 **380.6**km (236.5 ml) – Santiago de Compostela

TERRADILLOS de los Templarios *(Palencia)* **via SAHAGÚN** *(León)*
❶ BERCIANOS del Real Camino ❷ CALZADILLA de los Hermanillos

....	--- ---	19.6 --- ---	83%
	--- ---	3.7 --- ---	16%
▬▬▬	--- ---	0.2 --- ---	01%
Total km		**23.5** km (14.6 ml)	

▲ --- --- 23.5 km (+ 0 m)
Alto ▲ Terradillos 880m (2,890 ft)
<🅰 🏠> Moratinos **3.2** km – San Nicolás **6.0** km – Sahagún **13.0** km – Calzada
del Coto **18.3** km.

TERRADILLOS *880m*   *CALZADILLA*
900m Moratinos --- San Nicolás --- **SAHAGÚN** --- Calzada de Coto **BERCIANOS**
800m --- --- --- *Río Sequillo* --- *Río Cea*
00 km   5 km   10 km   15 km   20 km   25 km

▌ **Moratinos:** *Alb.*❶ Moratinos *Priv.[10÷2]+* €10 ✆ 979 061 466 c/ Real. *Alb.*
❷ **San Bruno** *Asoc.[16÷2]+* €7-9 ✆ 979 061 465 c/ Ontanón. ▌ **San Nicolás del
Real Camino** *(Palencia):* *Alb.* **Laganares** *Priv.*[20÷4]+ €9–€30 ✆ 979 188 142. ▌
SAHAGÚN *(León):* **p.64**

❶ *Real Camino* ● ● ● ● ▌ **Bercianos** *del Real Camino:* *Alb.* ❶ Bercianos *Par.
[46÷6]* €-donativo ✆ 987 784 008. ❷ **Santa Clara** *Priv.[10÷2]+* €10 + €25 Rosa
Fures ✆ 605 839 993 c/ Iglesia 3 / Plaza Mesón. *Hs* **Rivero** €25-35 ✆ 987 744 287.
❷ *Via Romana* ● ● ● ● ▌ **Calzada del Coto** *Alb.*San Roque *Muni.[36÷2]*
€-donativo ✆ 674 587 001 c/Real. ▌ **Calzadilla de los Hermanillos:** *Alb.* ❶ **Via
Trajana** *Priv.[20÷5]+* €15–€35 ✆ 987 337 610 c/Mayor + *menú.* ❷ **Calzadilla**
Muni.[22÷2] €-donativo ✆ 987 330 023. *HR*"Casa El Cura** €38-80 ✆ 987 337 647
c/La Carretera 13.

Real Camino ❶
Francesa

Via Romana ❷
Trajana

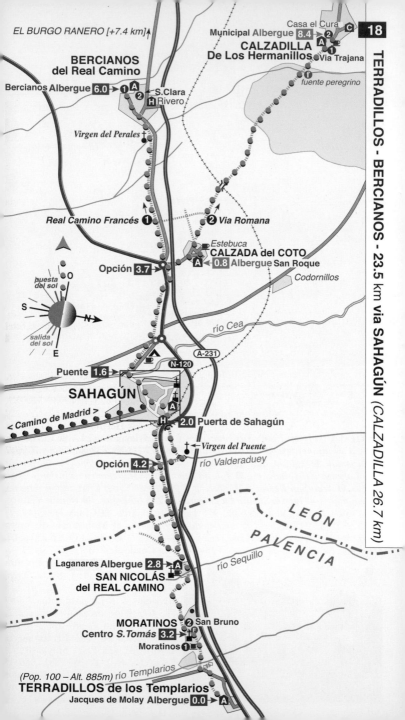

EL BURGO RANERO [+7.4 km]↑

BERCIANOS
del Real Camino

Casa el Cura
Municipal Albergue **8.4** ➋ **A** **C**
CALZADILLA
De Los Hermanillos
A ➊
Via Trajana

Bercianos Albergue **6.0** ➊ **A**
➋
H S.Clara
Rivero

fuente peregrino

Virgen del Perales †

Real Camino Francés ➊   ➋ *Via Romana*

Estebuca
CALZADA del COTO
Opción 3.7 →   **A** **0.8** Albergue San Roque

Codornillos

puesta del sol
O
S
salida del sol
E
N

río Cea

A-231
Puente 1.6 →   N-120

SAHAGÚN

< *Camino de Madrid* >

H **2.0** **Puerta de Sahagún**

† *Virgen del Puente*

Opción 4.2 →   *río Valderaduey*

LEÓN

PALENCIA

río Sequillo

Laganares Albergue **2.8** → **A**
SAN NICOLÁS
del REAL CAMINO

MORATINOS ➋ San Bruno
Centro *S.Tomás* **3.2**
Moratinos ➊

(Pop. 100 – Alt. 885m) río Templarios
TERRADILLOS de los Templarios
Jacques de Molay Albergue **0.0** → **A**

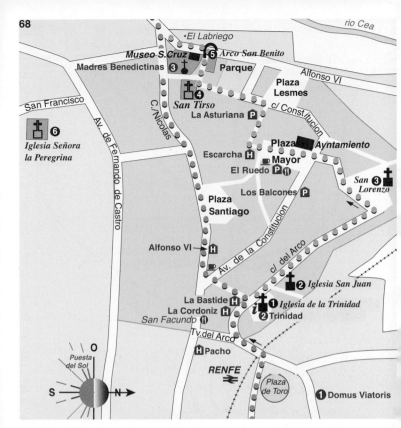

68

rio Cea

·El Labriego

Museo S.Cruz ❺ *Arco San Benito*

Madres Benedictinas ❸ **Parque**

Alfonso VI

Plaza Lesmes

❹ *San Tirso*

La Asturiana P

c/ Constitucion

C. Nicolas

San Francisco

Iglesia Señora la Peregrina ❻

Av. de Fernando de Castro

Plaza **Ayntamiento**

Escarcha H

Mayor ■

El Ruedo P

Los Balcones P

San Lorenzo ❸

Plaza Santiago

Alfonso VI — H

Av. de la Constitucion

c/ del Arco

❷ *Iglesia San Juan*

La Bastide H

La Cordoniz H

San Facundo

❶ *Iglesia de la Trinidad*

❷ **Trinidad**

Tv. del Arco

H **Pacho**

O
Puesta del Sol
S ← → **N**

RENFE

Plaza de Toro

❶ **Domus Viatoris**

■ **SAHAGÚN:** *(pop. 2,800) Turismo:* Iglesia de la Trinidad c/ del Arco ℂ 987 782 117. ❏ *Monumentos:* ❶ *Iglesia de la Trinidad XIII–XVII (municipal albergue + Turismo).* ❷ *Arco San Juan XVII (San Facundo y Primitivo).* ❸ *Iglesia San Lorenzo XII (Mudejar).* ❹ *Iglesia San Tirso (Mudejar ruinas)* Parque San Benito. ❺ *Arco San Benito* y **Monasterio y Museo de Santa Cruz** *museo (Madres Benedictinas).* ❻ *Iglesia Señora La Peregrina XV.* ■ *Albergues:* ❶ **Domus Viatoris** *Priv.**[50÷1]+ €7+€30 ℂ 987 780 975 Travesía del Arco. ❷ **Cluny** *Muni.[64÷1]* €5 ℂ 987 782 117 *(iglesia de la Trinidad y Turismo).* ❸ **Monasterio de Santa Cruz** *(Madres Benedictinas) Conv.[16÷4]+* €8 + €25. ℂ 987 781 139 c/ Nicolas 40. ■*Hoteles: Hs***Puerto de Sahagún* €25+. *Hs*** **La Cordoniz** €40 ℂ 987 780 276 c.

del Arco. *Hs* **La Bastide Du Chemin** €28 ℂ 987 781 183 c/ dcl Arco. *Hs***Alfonso VI €30 ℂ 987 781 144 c/Nicolás 4. *P* **La Asturiana** ℂ 987 780 073 Plaza de Lemses Franco 2 *Hs* **Don Pacho** ℂ 987 780 775 Av Constitución 84. *Hs** **El Ruedo I** ℂ 987 781 834 Plaza Mayor 1. *Hs* **Escarcha** €40 ℂ 987 781 856 c. Regina Franco 12. *P* **Los Balcones del Camino** €35 Juan Guaza 2 *(Av Constitución 53)* ℂ 676 838 242.

MANSILLA de las MULLAS

Arco de San Agustín

Plaza Picara Justina

C/ San Agustín

Museo Etnográfico
Plaza Convento

Los Cúbos

N

Centro Salud

c/ Noria

Molinos

León →

Las Delicias

El Puente
Alonso

Ayuntamiento

Plaza S. Nicolas
Municipal

Marcelo

Estación de Autobuses

c/ Mesones

Plaza del Pozo

c/ del Puente

La Curiosa

Plaza Grano

El Postigo

Dia%

❷ Gaia

Av. Constitución

c/Rioseco

Santa María

San Martín
Casa de Cultura

< Valladolid

Puerta Castillo

c/S. María

Alberguería

< c/Concepción

Plaza de la Leña

❶ El Jardín

Pensión Blanca P

Av. Picos de Europa

San Martín H

Arco de Santa María

Camping

rio Esla

MANSILLA DE LAS MULAS: *(pop: 1,900)* ❑ *Turismo* ✆ 987 310 012 Plaza del Pozo. *Convento de San Agustín Museo Etnográfico* c/ Agustín (10:00-14:00 / 16:00-19:00). *Alb.* ❶ **El Jardín del Camino** *Priv.[32÷2]*+ €8–€10+ ✆ 987 310 232 c/Camino de Santiago 1. ❷ **Gaia** *Priv.[18÷2]* €8 ✆ 987 310 308 m: 699 911 311 (Marisa) Av. Constitución 28. ❸ **Centro** *Muni.[76÷8]* €5 ✆ 661 977 305 c/ del Puente 5. *Hostales (centro): Rst.& Hs*° **El Puente** €35-€66 ✆ 987 310 075 c/ Mesones N°12. *& N°20-22 Rst'* & *Hs* **Las Delicias** €25-€40 ✆ 987 310 558. *Hs*°°° **Alberguería del Camino** €38 ✆ 987 311 193 c/Concepción, 12. *Otros: Pensión*° **Blanca** €25-60 ✆ 626 003 177 Av. Picos de Europa 4. *Hs*° **San Martín** €20+ ✆ 987 310 094 Av. Picos de Europa 32.

19 **357.1** km (221.9 ml) – Santiago

BERCIANOS — MANSILLA
del Real Camino   de las Mulas

....	--- ---	23.1	--- ---	87%
	--- ---	3.6	--- ---	13%
	--- ---	0.0	--- ---	0%
Total km		**26.7** km	(16.7 ml)	

	--- ---	26.7 km (+ 0 m)

Alto ▲ El Burgo Ranero 880m
< 🅰 🏠 > El Burgo Ranero **7.4** km – Reliegos **20.5** km.

BERCIANOS 850m   **El Burgo Ranero**
900m ■ *Calzadilla*   🅰   **Reliegos**
800m ─────────────── *río Valdecasa* ──────────────── 🅰 ── **MANSILLA** ■
            río Valdearco
```
00 km      5 km      10 km      15 km      20 km      25 km
```

❶ *Real Camino* ● ● ● ● **❙** **El Burgo Ranero:** *Alb.* **❶ Domenico Laffi** *Asoc.[28÷4]* €*-donativo* ✆ 987 330 023 c/Fray Pedro. **❷ El Nogal** *Asoc.[30÷8]* €7-10 ✆ 627 229 331. **❸ La Laguna** *Priv.[18÷1]*+ €9-25 ✆ 987 330 094 c/La Laguna *(Piedras Blancas)*. *Hs* **el Peregrino** €30 ✆ 987 330 069. *Hs* **Piedras Blancas** €30 ✆ 987 330 094. *Cafe El Camino (Paella!)* ✆ 674 58 39 47 c/ Real 53. **❙ Reliegos:** *Alb.* **❶ Piedras Blancas II** *Priv.[8÷2]*+ €9 -€45 ✆ 607 163 982. *Calle Real N°56* **❷ Vive tu Camino** *Priv.[20÷2]*+ €9 +€35 ✆ 987 317 837. *@N°42* **❸ Ada** ♥ *V. Priv.[20÷2]*+ €7 Vegetarian menú €8 ✆ 691 153 010 (Pedro) + *Sala de meditación. Centro Bar Gil II + Bar Elvis / La Torre (Sinín) [F.]* adj. **❹ Gil** *Priv.[12÷2]* ✆ 987 317 804 & bar. + 400m **❺ D.Gaiferos** *Muni.[45÷2]* €5 ✆ 987 317 801 c/Escuela adj. **❻ La Parada** *Priv.[36÷7]*+ €7 €30 ✆ 987 317 880 & bar. **❙ MANSILLA de las MULAS** *p.65.* **❷** *Via Romana* ● ● ● ● **❙** *Reliegos opción (+ 1.0 km).*

Reliegos:

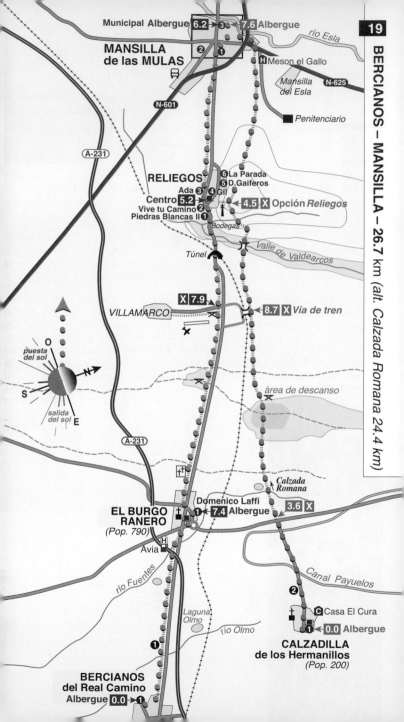

19

BERCIANOS – MANSILLA – 26.7 km (alt. Calzada Romana 24.4 km)

Municipal Albergue **6.2** → **3** → **7.6** Albergue

río Esla

MANSILLA de las MULAS

2 **1**

H Meson el Gallo

N-625

Mansilla del Esla

N-601

■ Penitenciario

A-231

RELIEGOS

6 La Parada

5 D.Gaiferos

Ada **3** **4** Gil

Centro **5.2** →

4.5 **X** Opción *Reliegos*

2

Vive tu Camino

Piedras Blancas II **1**

Bodegas

Túnel

Valle de Valdearcos

X **7.9** →

VILLAMARCO

8.7 **X** *Vía de tren*

puesta del sol

O

N

S

E salida del sol

área de descanso

A-231

Calzada Romana

Domenico Laffi **1** **7.4** Albergue

3.6 **X**

EL BURGO RANERO

(Pop. 790)

H

Avia

río Fuentes

Canal Payuelos

2

Laguna Olmo

río Olmo

C Casa El Cura

1 **0.0** Albergue

CALZADILLA de los Hermanillos

(Pop. 200)

BERCIANOS del Real Camino

Albergue **0.0** → **1**

20 **330.4** km (205.3 ml) – Santiago

MANSILLA de las MULAS ❸ – LEÓN ❷

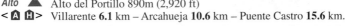

⋯⋯⋯⋯	--- ---	10.2	--- --- 56%
▬▬	--- ---	3.5	--- --- 20%
▬▬	--- ---	4.4	--- --- 24%
Total km		**18.1** km (11.2 ml)	

◣ --- --- 18.6 km (+ 0.5 km)
Alto ▲ Alto del Portillo 890m (2,920 ft)
< **Ⓐ Ⓗ** > Villarente **6.1** km – Arcahueja **10.6** km – Puente Castro **15.6** km.

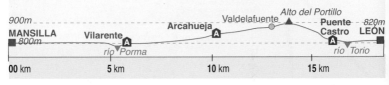

■ Puente Villarente: *Alb.* **❶ Hospedería Filosofía** *Priv.[10÷1]+* €8+€15 ✆ 602 073 335 (< Casa Blanca). **❷ El Delfín Verde** *Priv.[30]* ✆ 987 312 065. **❸ San Pelayo** *Priv.*[56÷4]+* €8 ✆ 987 312 677. *Hs°* **La Montaña** ✆ 987 312 161 N-601. **■Arcahueja:** *Alb.* **La Torre** *Priv.[26÷3]+* €8 +€25 ✆ 987 205 896. **■ Valdelafuente:** *Hs°°°* **Camino Real** ✆ 987 218 134 (+300m). **■ Puente Castro:** *Alb.* **Santo Tomás de Canterbury** *Priv.[60÷8]* €8 ✆ 987 392 626 Av. de La Lastra *(Citroën).* **Check in León** *Priv.[40÷2]* €10 ✆ 987 498 793 Alcalde Miguel Castaño 88. **■ LEÓN** *p.74*

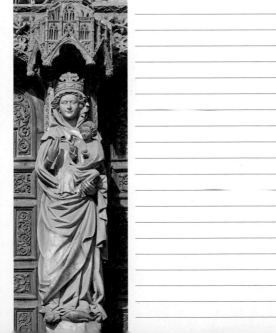

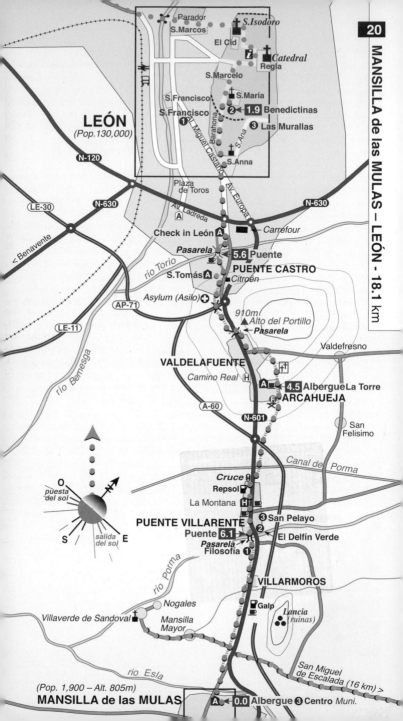

Parador
S.Marcos
S.Isodoro
El Cid
Catedral
Regla
S.Marcelo
S.Maria
S.Francisco
S.Francisco **1**
2 **1.9** Benedictinas
3 Las Murallas
Barahona
S.Ana
S.Anna
Miguel Castaño

LEÓN
(Pop.130,000)

N-120
LE-30
N-630
N-630

Plaza de Toros
Av. Europa
Av. Ladreda
Check in León
Carrefour
Pasarela **5.6** Puente
PUENTE CASTRO
S.Tomás
Citroën
río Torío

Asylum (Asilo)
AP-71
910m
LE-11
Alto del Portillo
Pasarela

Valdefresno

VALDELAFUENTE
Camino Real
4.5 AlbergueLa Torre
ARCAHUEJA

A-60
N-601

San Felismo

Canal de Porma

Cruce
Repsol
La Montana
3 San Pelayo
PUENTE VILLARENTE
Puente **6.1**
2
El Delfín Verde
Pasarela
Filosofia **1**

VILLARMOROS

Galp
Lancia (ruinas)

río Bernesga

O
puesta del sol
S
E
salida del sol

río Porma

Nogales
Villaverde de Sandoval
Mansilla Mayor
San Miguel de Escalada (16 km) >

río Esla

(Pop. 1,900 – Alt. 805m)
MANSILLA de las MULAS
0.0 Albergue **3** Centro *Muni.*

< Benavente

74

LEÓN *(pop: 130,000)* **Centro:** ❏ *Turismo:* Plaza Regla (Catedral) ✆ 987 237 082
+ *Turistica Info.* Plaza S.Marcelo *Ayuntamiento Viejo.* ❏ *Credencial Asociación de
Amigos del Camino* Av. Independencia, 5º ✆ 987 260 530 / 677 430 200. *Equipos
peregrino y guias:* Armería Castro c/La Rúa 7 ✆ 987 257 020.
❏ *Monumentos históricos:* ❶ *Puerta Moneda (muralla romana)* ❷ *Iglesia de S.
María del camino* (Mercado) *XII.* ❸ *Iglesia S.Marcelo XII - XVII.* ❹ *Casa Botines
(Gaudí).* ❺ *Palacio Guzmanes XVI (+ patio).* ❻ *Catedral Pulchra Leonina XIII
(museo + claustro).* ❼ *Basilica de San Isidoro XII (Misa del peregrino 19:30).* ❽
Panteón Real XI. ❾ *San Marcos (Museo / Parador / Claustro XII– XVI).*

∎ *Albergues: Alb.* ❶ **San Francisco de Asís** *Residencia Fundación Ademar Asoc.
[166÷47]* €10-18 ✆ 637 439 848 Av. Alcalde Miguel Castaños, 4 (adj. *Jardin San
Franciso).* ❷ **S.María de Carbajal** *Conv.[132÷4]* €5 ✆ 987 252 866 *Plaza Grano
/ Santa María del Camino).* ❸ **Muralla Leonesa** *Priv.[70÷20]* €10-€35 ✆ 987 177
873 c/ Tarifa 5. ❹ *Hs* **Urban Rio Cea** *Priv.[8÷2]+* €15-18+€50+ ✆ 636 946 294
c/ Legión VII, 6/ 2º *(adj. Ayuntamiento Viejo).* ❺ **LeonHostel** *Priv.[20÷4]+* €12-
15+€30 ✆ 987 079 907 c/ Ancha 8 adj. Catedral. ❻ **Unamuno** *Priv.[86÷16]* €10-20
c/ San Pelayo, 15 ✆ 987 233 010 *residencia Universitaria Unamuno.* ∎ *Hoteles*
€30-€60*: P*º**Sandoval** ✆ 987 212 041 c/Hospicio, 11-2º. *H*ººº **Monástica Pax** ✆
987 344 493 Plaza Grano, 11. *H*ººº **Toral** ✆ 987 207 738 Cuesta de las Carbajalas.
*H*º **Rincón del Conde** ✆ 987 849 021 Conde Rebolledo. *Hr*ººº**La Posada Regia
I & II** ✆ 987 213 173 c/Regidores, 9. *H*ººº **París** ✆ 987 238 600 c/Ancha, 18.
*HsR*º**Albany** ✆ 987 264 600 La Paloma,13. *H*ººº **Le Petit Leon** ✆ 987 075 508 c/
Del Pozo, 2. *H*ºººº**NH Plaza Mayor** ✆ 987 344 357 Plaza Mayor,15. *P*º **Puerta Sol**
P ✆ 987 211 966 c/Puerta Sol,1. ∎ *adj. Cathedral: H*ººº **QH** ✆ 987 875 580 Av.Los
Cubos,6. *Hs*ºº**Fernando I** ✆ 987 220 601 Av.Los Cubos,32. *Hs*ºº **Casco Antiguo** ✆
987 074 000 c/Cardenal Landázuri,11. *HsR*º **Guzmán el Bueno** ✆ 987 236 412 c/
López Castrillón, 6. *HsR*º **San Martín** ✆ 987 875 187 Plaza Torres de Omaña, 1.
*Hs*ºº**Boccalino** ✆ 987 223 060 plaza S. Isodoro, 9. *HsR*ºº **Boccalino II** ✆ 987 220
017 Plaza S. Isodoro, 1. *H*ººº **Casa de Espiritualidad (S.Idodoro)** ✆ 987 875 088
Plaza Santo Martino. ∎ *Otros: Hr*º **Reina** ✆ 987 205 212 c/Puerta de la Reina, 2.
*HsR*º**Alvarez** ✆ 987 072 520 c/Burgo Nuevo, 3. *H*ººº**Alfonso V** Sercotel ✆ 987-220
900 Av. Padre Isla, 1. *HsR*º **Padre Isla II** ✆ 987 228 097 Av.Padre Isla, 8. *HsR*º
Padre Isla ✆ 987 092 298 Joaquín Costa,2. *H*ºº **La Torre S. Isidoro** c/Torre, 3, ✆
987 225 594. ∎ *adj. Estación de tren: H*ºº **Orejas** ✆ 987 252 909 c/Villafranca, 8.
*P*º**Blanca** ✆ 987 2521 991 c/Villafranca, 2. *H*º **Londres** ✆ 987-222 274 Av. Roma,
1. *HsR*ºº **Don Suero** ✆ 987 230 600 Av. Suero de Quiñones, 15. *H*ººººº **Parador San
Marcos** €90+ ✆ 987 237 300 adj. *Hs*ºº**Quevedo** €29! ✆ 987 242 975 Av. Quevedo.

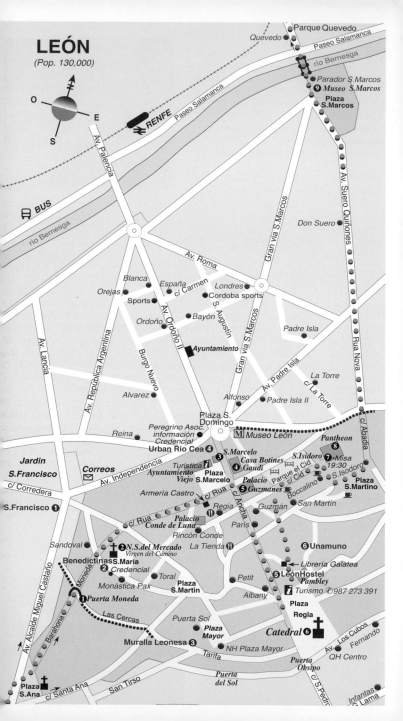

21 312.3 km (194.1 ml) – Santiago

LEÓN – VILLADANGOS del PÁRAMO
Alt. VILLAR DE MAZARIFE

::::::::::	--- --- 9.8	--- --- 46%
▬▬▬	--- --- 5.4	--- --- 25%
▬▬▬	--- --- 6.1	--- --- 29%
Total km	**21.3** km (13.2 ml)	

21.9 km (^250m +0.6 km)
Alto ▲ Páramo 901m (2,956 ft)
<**Ⓐ Ⓗ**> Virgen del Camino **8.5** km – Valverde – **11.9** km.

```
                                                      Chozas
900m          Alto Cruceiro  La Virgen  Valverde  S.Miguel  de Abajo    MAZARIFE
 LEÓN                          Ⓐ        Ⓐ        ▢                  ▢  VILLADANGOS
800m                                          Río Oncina
 00 Km         5 km          10 km            15 km               20 km
```

▮ **Trobajo del Camino:** *Alb.* **Casa Simón** *Priv.[32÷2]*+ €16 B&B +25 ✆ 987 807 552 c/de Guzmán El Bueno, 52. ▮ **LA VIRGEN DEL CAMINO N-120** *H*** **VillaPaloma** €35 ✆ 987 300 990. *Hs* **Julio Cesar** ✆ 987 302 044 c/Cervantes. *Hs* **San Froilán** ✆ 987 302 019 / *Hs*** **Plaza** €27 c/Peregrino. *Hs* **Central** ✆ 987 302 041. *Alb.* **D.Antonino y Dña.Cinia** *Muni.[40÷1]* €5 ✆ 615 217 335 c/Camino de Villacedré *(adj. Seminario on Av. Padre Eustoquio).* ❶ ● ● ● *Via Mazarife:* **Mazarife:** *Alb.* ❶ **San Antonio de Pádua** *Priv.[50÷1]*+ €8-€30 ✆ 987 390 192. ❷ *Casa de Jesús Priv.[50÷10]* €5 ✆ 686 053 390. ❸ **Tio Pepe** *Priv.[22÷4]*+ €9-€40. ❷ ● ● ● *Via Villadangos:* ▮ **Valverde de la Virgen:** *Alb.* **La Casa del Camino** *Priv.[32÷1]* €8 ✆ 669 874 750 (Alejandra) c/ El Jano, 2 / N-120. ▮ **Villadangos del Páramo:** *Hr*** **Avenida III** ✆ 987 390 311 N-120. *Alb.* **Villadangos** *Asoc.[54÷7]* €5 ✆ 987 102 910. *Hs*** **Libertad** ✆ 987 390 123 N-120.

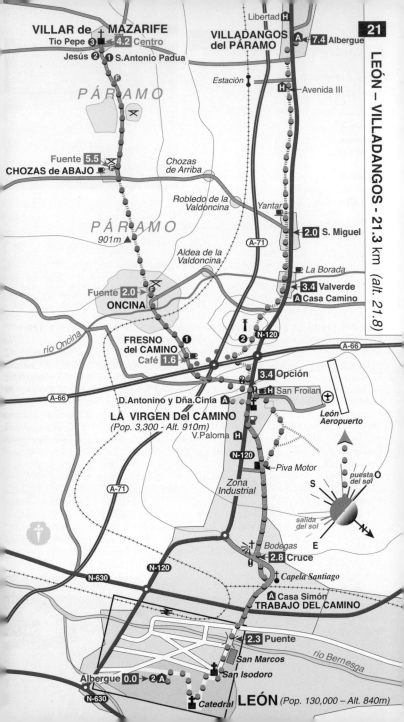

VILLAR de MAZARIFE
Tio Pepe ❸ ■ ◀4.2 Centro
Jesús ❷ ❶ S.Antonio Padua

PÁRAMO

Fuente 5.5
CHOZAS de ABAJO

Chozas de Arriba

Robledo de la Valdoncina

PÁRAMO
901m ▲

Aldea de la Valdoncina

Fuente 2.0
ONCINA

FRESNO del CAMINO ❶
Café 1.6

A-66

D.Antonino y Dña.Cinia Ⓐ

LA VIRGEN Del CAMINO
(Pop. 3,300 - Alt. 910m)

V.Paloma Ⓗ

N-120

Zona Industrial

A-71

N-630

N-120

Albergue 0.0 ❷Ⓐ

Libertad Ⓗ
VILLADANGOS del PÁRAMO
Ⓐ ◀7.4 Albergue

Estación
Ⓗ Avenida III

Yantar
2.0 S. Miguel

La Borada
3.4 Valverde
Ⓐ Casa Camino

A-71

N-120 ❷

3.4 Opción

ⒽSan Froilan
⊕
León Aeropuerto

Piva Motor

puesta del sol
S
O
salida del sol
E

Bodegas
◀2.8 Cruce

Capela Santiago

Ⓐ Casa Simón
TRABAJO DEL CAMINO

2.3 Puente
río Bernesga
San Marcos
San Isodoro

Catedral LEÓN (Pop. 130,000 – Alt. 840m)

22 **291.0** km (180.8 ml) – Santiago

VILLADANGOS – ASTORGA
Alt. MAZARIFE – PUENTE DE ÓRBIGO

⋯⋯⋯⋯⋯	--- ---	22.2	--- ---	78%
▬▬▬	--- ---	5.8	--- ---	20%
▬▬	--- ---	0.5	--- ---	02%
Total km		**28.5** km	(17.7 ml)	

🔺 --- --- 29.7 (^250m+1.2 km)
Alto ▲ Santo Toribio 905m (2,970 ft).

<**Ⓐ Ⓗ**> San Martín **4.7** km – Hospital de Órbigo **11.3** km – Villares **14.4** km Santibáñez **16.9** km – San Justo **24.9** km.
Alt. via Mazarife / Páramo – Villavante 9.9 km.

```
                                                    Alto S.Toribio
MAZARIFE  S.Martín                    HOSPITAL            925m    ASTORGA
         Ⓐ          Villavante      DEL ÓRBIGO  Santibañez      ▲
    VILLADANGOS   Ⓐ                    Ⓐ          Ⓐ         S.Justo  870m
800m                            Río Órbigo
00 km      5 km      10 km      15 km      20 km      25 km      30
```

❶ ● ● ● *Via Mazarife:* **Villavante:** *Alb.* **Santa Lucía** *Priv.[24÷1]*+ €8–€28 ℭ 692 107 693 c/ Doctor Vélez. *CR* **Molino Galochas** ℭ 987 388 546.
❷ ● ● ● *Via Villadangos:* ∎ **San Martín del Camino:** *N-120:* *Alb.* ❶ **Vieira** *Priv. [40÷8]* €7 ℭ 987 378 565. ❷ **Santa Ana** *Priv.[64÷3]*+ €6+20 987 039 322 (Patri & Xavi). ❸ **La Casa Verde** *Priv.[8÷1]* €10 ℭ 646 879 437 (Beatriz Puente) Trv. de La Estación 8. ❹ **San Martín** *Muni.[68÷2]* €5 ℭ 616 354 331. ∎ **Puente de Órbigo:** *P* **Fonda Alicia** ℭ 987 388 349. *P* **Lar la Puente** ℭ 987 361 100. **La Casa de la Inspiración** *Asoc.[12÷2]* €5 ℭ 622 636 856 (Felipe y Verónica) c/ Paso Honroso 10 ∎ **HOSPITAL DE ÓRBIGO:** *Alb.* ❶ **La Encina** *Priv.[16÷4]*+ €9-36 ℭ 987 361 087 Av. de Suero de Quinoñes. ● **camping** *municipal.* *Hs**Don Suero de Quiñones ℭ 987 388 238. ❷ **Karl Leisner** *Par.[90÷10]* €5 ℭ 987 388 444. ❸ **San Miguel** *Asoc.*[40÷2]* €7 ℭ 987 388 285. ❹ **Verde** *Priv.[26÷2]* V. €9 ℭ 689 927 926 Av. Fueros de León (+500m /N-120). *CR* **N.S. de Lourdes** €20-40 ℭ 987 388 253 / 639 001 024 c/Sierra Pambley, 40. *CR* **El Caminero** €50+ ℭ 987 389 020 c/ Sierra Pambley, 56. *H* **El Paso Honroso** €35 ℭ 987 361 010 N-120 *(adj. gasolinera Cepsa).* ∎ **Villares de Órbigo:** *Alb.* **Villares Casa de Pablo y Belén** *Priv.[26÷5]*+ €7–€20 ℭ 947 132 935. ∎ **Santibáñez de Valdeiglesia:** *Alb.* ❶ **Santibáñez** *Par. [20÷4]* €5 ℭ 626 362 159 *(adj. bar Centro Social).* ❷ **Camino Francés** *Priv.[12÷2]* ℭ 987 361 014 c/ Real. ∎ **San Justo de la Vega:** *Alb.* **Amanecer** *Plgrim House Priv. [11÷3] donativo* ℭ 622 566 468 cena comunitaria. *HsR** **Juli** ℭ 987 617 632.

Puente de Órbigo:

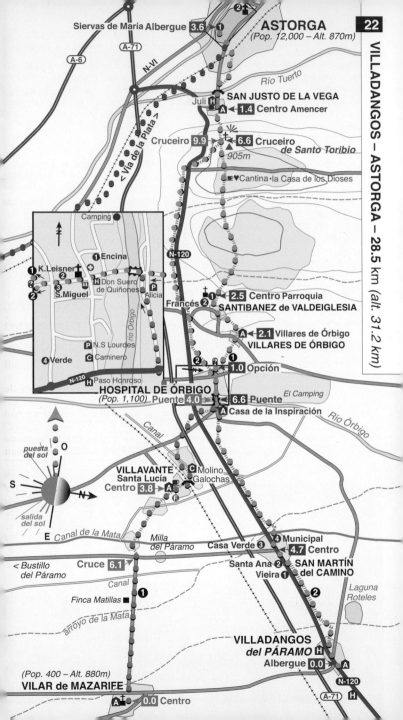

Siervas de María Albergue **3.6** ❶

ASTORGA
(Pop. 12,000 – Alt. 870m)

A-6

A-71

N-VI

Río Tuerto

SAN JUSTO DE LA VEGA
Juli Ⓗ
Ⓐ ◄ **1.4** Centro Amencer

Cruceiro **9.9** → ✝ **6.6** Cruceiro
de Santo Toribio
▲ *905m*

> *Vía de la Plata* <

■♥ Cantina • la Casa de los Dioses

Camping

❶ Encina

K.Leisner ✝
❶
❷
?
❷ S.Miguel
Ⓗ Don Suero
de Quiñones
Ⓟ
Alicia

N-120

✝ ❶ **2.5** Centro Parroquia
❷ **SANTIBANEZ de VALDEIGLESIA**
Francés

Ⓐ **2.1** Villares de Órbigo
VILLARES DE ÓRBIGO

❷ ? ❶ **1.0** Opción

Ⓟ N.S Lourdes
Ⓒ Caminero

❹ Verde

N-120

Ⓗ Paso Honroso
HOSPITAL DE ÓRBIGO
(Pop. 1,100) Puente **4.0** ✝ **6.6** Puente
El Camping

Ⓐ Casa de la Inspiración
Río Órbigo

Canal

*puesta
del sol*

O

S ☀ N

*salida
del sol*

E Canal de la Mata

Ⓒ Molino
Galochas
VILLAVANTE
Santa Lucía
Centro **3.8** Ⓐ
Ⓕ

Milla
del Páramo
Casa Verde ❸ ❹ Municipal
4.7 Centro
Santa Ana ❷ **SAN MARTÍN**
Vieira ❶ **del CAMINO**

Cruce **6.1** ↗
< Bustillo
del Páramo

Canal

Finca Matillas ■ ❶

❷

*Laguna
Roteles*

arroyo de la Mata

VILLADANGOS
del PÁRAMO Ⓗ
Albergue **0.0** Ⓐ

N-120

A-71 Ⓗ

(Pop. 400 – Alt. 880m)
VILAR de MAZARIFE
Ⓐ ✝ ● **0.0** Centro

■ **ASTORGA:** *(pop: 12,000)* ❏ *Turismo:* ✆ 987 618 222 Glorieta Eduardo Castro, 5. ❏ *Monumentos:* ❶ *Plaza San Francisco Convento de San Francisco / Murallas Romano (ruinas).* ❷ *Plaza Bartolomé Iglesia San Bartolomé / Ergástula (museo).* ❸ *Plaza Mayor (Plaza España) Ayuntamiento.* ❹ *Plaza Santocildes Museo del Chocolate.* ❺ *Plaza Obispo Alcolea Puerta de Rey / Casa Granell.* ❻ *Plaza Catedral Palacio Episcopal* (Gaudí) *Museo de los Caminos* y *Cruz de Ferro / Iglesia de Santa Marta / Catedral XV Museo de Catedral.*

■ *Albergues:* ❶ **Siervas de María** *Asoc.[164÷20]* €5 ✆ 987 616 034 Plaza San Francisco. ❷ **San Javier** *Asoc.*[95÷5]* €9 ✆ 987 618 532 c/Portería, 6. ■ *Hostales:* (€45-65)*:* H^{**} **La Peseta** ✆ 987 617 275 Plaza San Bartolomé. adj. H^{****} **Vía De La Plata** c/Padres Redentoristas, 5 €100 ✆ 987 619 000. H^{***} **Astvr Plaza** ✆ 987 617 665 Plaza Mayor (España). *P* **García** ✆ 987 616 046 c/Bajada Postigo. **Casa de Tepa** ✆ 987 603 299 c/Santiago,2. H^{***}**Ciudad De Astorga Spa** ✆ 987 603 001 c/ los Sitios,7. Hr^{***}**El Descanso de Wendy** ✆ 987 617 854 c/ Matadero Viejo, 11. H^{***} **Gaudí** ✆ 987 615 654 Plaza Catedral. Hr^{**}**Gallego** ✆ 987 615 450 Av. Ponferrada. *H* **Coruña** ✆ 987 615 009.

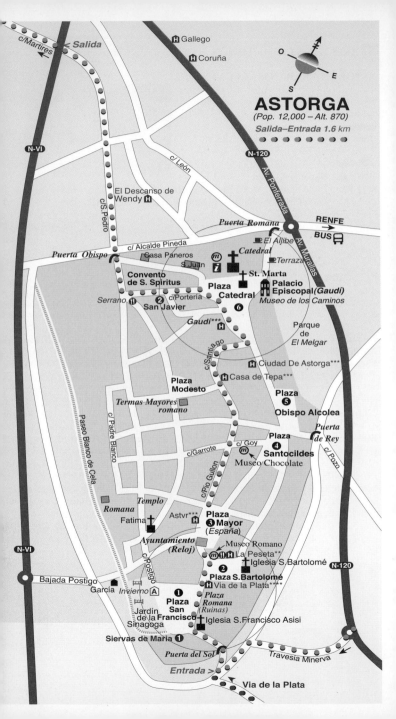

23 262.5 km (163.1 ml) – Santiago

ASTORGA – RABANAL del CAMINO

⫫⫫⫫⫫⫫⫫	--- ---	14.1	--- ---	68%
▬▬▬▬	--- ---	6.5	--- ---	32%
▬▬	--- ---	0.0	--- ---	
Total km		**20.6** km (12.8 ml)		

◣◢ --- --- 22.6 km (^400m+2.0)
Alto ▲ Rabanal 1,150m (3,770 ft)
< Ⓐ Ⓗ > *from albergue* ❶*:* Murias de Rechivaldo **5.1** km *[Castrillo Polvazares 7.3 km off route]* – Santa Catalina **9.4** km – El Ganso **13.7** km.

Elevation profile:
1,100m — 1,155m **RABANAL** ■
1,000m — Santa Catalina Ⓐ — Ganso Ⓐ — Arroyo
900m — **Murias de Rechivalda** Ⓐ — Castrillo Ⓐ — Arroyo
ASTORGA ■ — *Río Jerga*
800m —
00 km | 5 km | 10 km | 15 km | 20 km

❚ **Valdeviejas:** *Alb.* **Ecce Homo** *Muni.[10÷2]* €5 ✆ 620 960 060. ❚ **Murias de Rechivaldo:** *Alb.* ❶ **Casa las Águedas** *Priv.[40÷3]*+€9 +€45 ✆ 636 067 840. ❷ **La Escuela** *Muni.[14÷1]* €5 ✆ 987 691 150. ❸ **Casa Flor** *Priv.[15÷3]*+ €10 (€20 incl.) ✆ 609 478 323. **La Valeta** ✆ 616 598 133 Plaza Mayor. ●**Castrillo de Polvazares:** *Alb.* **Municipal.***[8÷2]* €5 ✆ 655 803 706 (Rubén García) c/ del Jardín. *Hs* **Don Álvaro** ✆ 987 053 990 c/ La Magdalena. *Hs* **Cuca La Vaina** €45 ✆ 987-691 034 c/ del Jardin. *CR* **Casa Coscolo** €45 c/El rincon (Plaza de la iglesia). ❚ **Santa Catalina:** *Alb.* ❶ **El Caminante** *Priv.[16÷2]*+ €5 ✆ 987 691 098. *Alb.* ❷ **Hospedería San Blas** *Priv.[20÷2]*+ €5-€35 ✆ 987 691 411. ❚ **El Ganso** *Alb.* **Gabino** *Priv.[30÷3]* €8 ✆ 660 912 823. ❚ **Rabanal del Camino:** *Apartamentos* **Las Carballedas** €60 ✆ 686 705 595. **c/ Real:** *Posada* **El Tesín** €35 ✆ 635 527 522 adj. *Alb.* ❶ **La Senda** *Priv.[34÷4]* €5–€7 ✆ 696 819 060. *H* **Casa Indie** €40-60 ✆ 625 470 392 c/ del Medio 4a. *CR* **A Cruz de Ferro** €30-40 ✆ 627 147 115. *Alb.* ❷ **Gaucelmo** *Asoc. [40÷3]* €-donativo ✆ 987 631 647. *Iglesia de la Santa María XII misa del peregrino* 19:00. ● **Benedictine Monasterio** *San Salvador del Monte Irago* €-donativo ✆ 987 631 528. *Hs* **Meson El Refugio** €35-50 ✆ 987 631 592. *H***La Posada de Gaspar** €55 ✆ 987 631 629. Plaza Gerónimo Morán Alonso ❸ **N.S del Pilar** *Priv.[32÷2]*+ €5 +35 ✆ 987 631 621. ❹ *Muni.[34÷2]* €4 ✆ 987 631 687.

_____
_____
_____
_____
_____
_____
_____
_____

Gaspar
Salida
Monasterio
Mesón
El Refugio
S.María
Pilar 3
2
Gaucelmo
Gaudisse
c/Medio
c/Medio
Indie
Municipal 4
c/Abajo
c/Abajo
0.6 km
Cruz de Ferro
c/Real
Camping
La Senda 1
El Tesín
RABANAL del CAMINO
Entrada
(Pop. 50 – Alt. 1,160m)
RABANAL del CAMINO
2.8 Centro S.María
Rabanal Viejo
Ermita del Bendito Cristo
Las Carballedas
La Fucarona (Minas Romanas)
Via Crucis
roble 1713–2013!
4.1 Puente de Pañote
Santa Colomba de Somoza
Casa Pepa
Gabino
El Ganso 4.3
Cowboy Bar
río Jerga
río Turienzo
Hospedería San Blas
2
SANTA CATALINA de SOMOZA
Centro 2.0
1 El Caminante
O
puesta del sol
N
S
salida del sol
E
Don Álvaro
Municipal
X 2.3
Cuca la Vaina
2.0 Castrillo de Polvazares
A-6
N-120
Las Águedas 1
3 Casa Flor
2 La Escuela
Centro 2.0
MURIAS de RECHIVALDO
Puente
3.1 Puente A-6
Ecce Homo
Ecce Homo
VALDEVIEJAS
St. Javier*
2
Catedral
A-6
(Pop. 12,000 – Alt. 870m)
Albergue 1 0.0
ASTORGA

24 **241.9** km (150.3 ml) – Santiago

RABANAL del CAMINO – MOLINASECA

⠿⠿⠿⠿⠿	--- ---	20.6	--- ---	80%
	--- ---	4.5	--- ---	18%
▬▬▬	--- ---	0.5	--- ---	2%
Total km		**25.6** km (15.9 ml)		

▲▲ --- --- 28.6 km (^600m + 3.0 km)
Alto ▲ La Cruz de Ferro 1,505m (4,940 ft)
<Ⓐ Ⓗ> Foncebadón **5.8** km – Manjarín **9.7** km
Acebo **16.5** – Riego de Ambros **19.9** km.

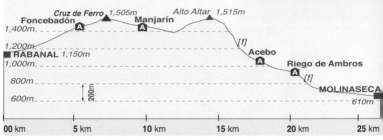

■ **Foncebadón:** *Alb.* ❶ **Roger de Lauri** *Priv.[20÷2]* €7 ✆ 625 313 425. ❷ **Monte Irago** *Priv.[22÷3]* €5 ✆ 695 452 950. ❸ **Domus Dei** *Par.[18÷1]* €-*donativo*. ❹ **La Posada del Druida** *Priv.[20÷3]* €7 ✆ 696 820 136. ❺ **La Cruz de Fierro** *Priv. [36÷2]* €7 ✆ 669 752 144. *P* **El Trasgu** €25-35 ✆ 987 053 877 y mercado.
■ **Manjarín** *Alb.* **Manjarín** *Priv.[35]* €-*donativo*. ■ **Acebo:** *c/Real: Alb.* ❶ **Elisardo Panizo** *Muni.[10÷1]*. ❷ **Mesón El Acebo** *Priv.[18÷1]*+ €7-24 ✆ 987 695 074. ❸ **Taberna de José** *Priv.[7÷2]*. ❹ **Apóstol Santiago** *Par.[23÷1]* €-*donativo*. ❺ **La Casa del Peregrino** *[96÷8]*+ €10-50 ✆ 987 057 793 c/Compludo. *Hostales:* (€40+)*: CR* **La Rosa del Agua** *La Tienda* ✆ 616 849 738. *CR* **La Casa del Peregrino** ✆ 987 057 875. *CR* **La Casa Monte Irago** ✆ 639 721 242. *Hs* **Mesón El Acebo**. *CR* **La Trucha** ✆ 987 695 548. ■ **Riego de Ambros:** *Alb.* **Riego de Ambros** *Muni.[30÷2]* €5 ✆ 987 695 190. *P* **Riego de Ambros** €20-35 ✆ 987 695 188.
■ **MOLINASECA** €25-55: *HsR******* **El Palacio** ✆ 987 453 094. *Hs* **The Way** ✆ 637 941 017 c/El Palacio. *Hs* **El Horno** ✆ 987 453 203 m: 627 554 260 c/El Rañadero 3. *CR* **San Nicolas** ✆ 645 652 008 C/ La iglesia 43. *c/Real: CR* **El Reloj** ✆ 987 453 124. *CR* **Pajarapinta** ✆ 987 453 040. *Hs* **Posada de Muriel** ✆ 987 453 201. *P.* **Casa Pichín** ✆ 655 469 017 Trav. Manuel Fraga,17. / *Av. Fraga Ibibarne:H*********Floriana** €15–€55 ✆ 987 453 146. / **+ ½ km:** *Alb.* ❶ **Santa Marina** *Priv.*[56÷5]* €7 ✆ 987 453 077. ❷ **San Roque** *Mun.[26÷1]* €5.

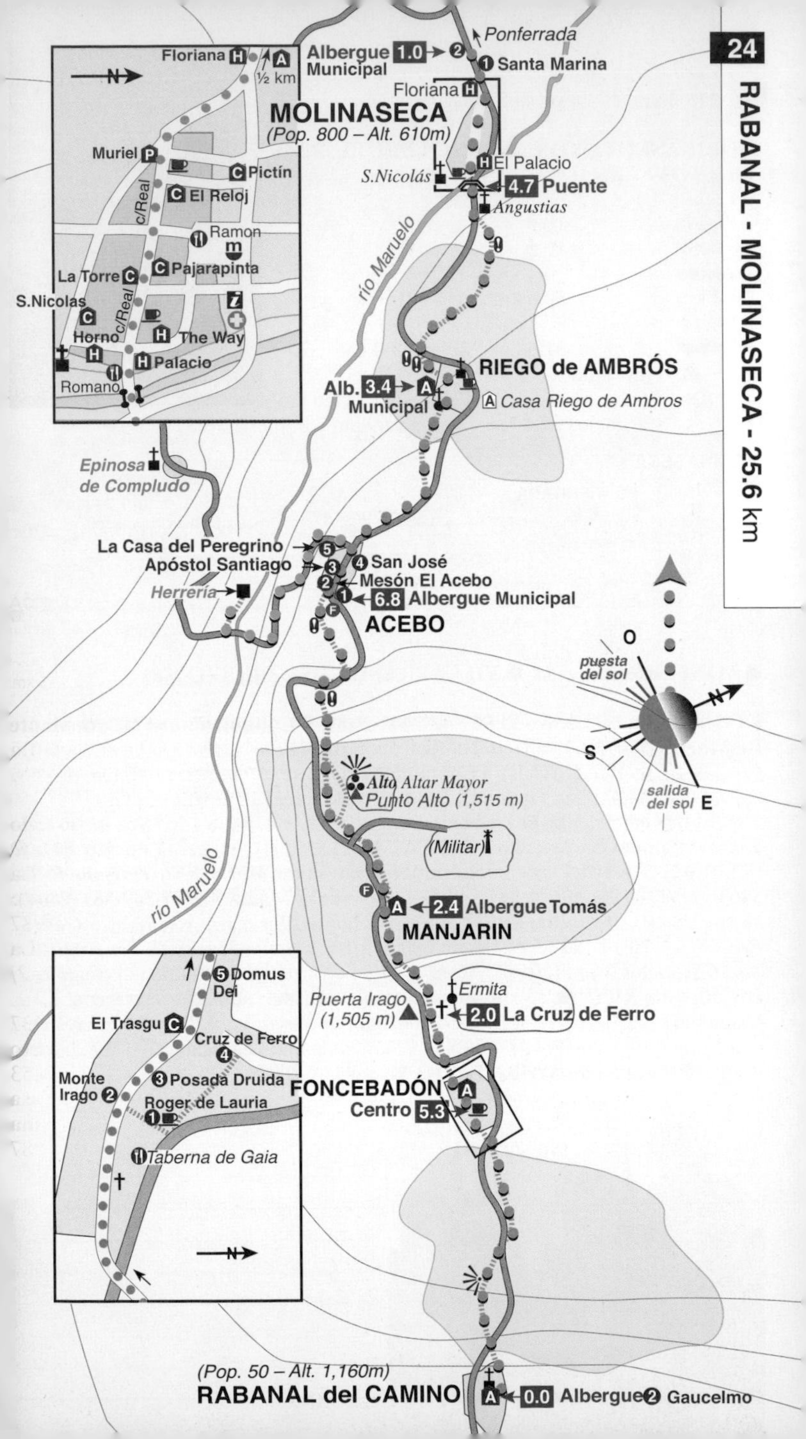

↑ *Ponferrada*

Albergue **1.0** ② ❶ Santa Marina
Municipal
Floriana Ⓗ

Floriana Ⓗ ↗ Ⓐ
½ km

MOLINASECA
(Pop. 800 – Alt. 610m)

Ⓗ El Palacio
S.Nicolás ❙ ◄ **4.7** Puente
Angustias

Muriel Ⓟ
Ⓒ Pictín
Ⓒ El Reloj
❶ Ramon
m
Ⓒ Pajarapinta

La Torre Ⓒ
S.Nicolas
Ⓘ
Ⓗ The Way

Ⓗ **Horno**
Ⓗ **Palacio**
Romano ✝

rio Maruelo

θθ

RIEGO de AMBRÓS

Alb. **3.4** Ⓐ
Municipal Ⓐ *Casa Riego de Ambros*

Epinosa ✝
de Compludo

La Casa del Peregrino → ⑤
Apóstol Santiago → ③ ❹ San José
Herreria ▪ ② ← Mesón El Acebo
❶ Ⓕ **6.8** Albergue Municipal
θ **ACEBO**

θ

☀ *Alto Altar Mayor*
✝ *Punto Alto (1,515 m)*

(Militar) ✝

rio Maruelo

Ⓕ Ⓐ ← **2.4** Albergue Tomás
MANJARIN

✝ *Ermita*
Puerta Irago ▲ ✝ **2.0** La Cruz de Ferro
(1,505 m)

FONCEBADÓN Ⓐ
Centro **5.3**

⑤Domus
Dei
El Trasgu Ⓒ
Cruz de Ferro
Monte ④
Irago② ③ Posada Druida
❶ Roger de Lauria
❶ *Taberna de Gaia*
✝

(Pop. 50 – Alt. 1,160m)
RABANAL del CAMINO Ⓐ ← **0.0** Albergue② Gaucelmo

O
puesta del sol
S
E
salida del sol

25 **216.3** km (134.4 ml) – Santiago

MOLINASECA – VILLAFRANCA DEL BIERZO
(via PONFERRADA)

⋯⋯⋯⋯	--- ---	10.0 --- ---	33%
▬▬▬	--- ---	16.5 --- ---	54%
▬▬▬	--- ---	4.1 --- ---	13%
Total km		**30.6** km (19.0 ml)	

31.6 km (^200m +1.0 km)
Alto ▲ Alto Villafranca 550m (1,805 ft)
< **A H** > Ponferrada **5.3** km – Camponarya **16.6** km
Cacabelos **22.0** km – Pieros **24.9** km – Valtuille **26.3** km.

MOLINASECA
```
     600m                                                          Alto
              PONFERRADA                                          605m
                                                              VILLAFRANCA
     500m         A                  Camponaraya      Cacabelos  A      570m
          Río Boeza   Río Sil                              A Pieros
     400m                                          Río Cúa

00 km      5 km      10 km      15 km      20 km      25 km      30 km
```

■ **PONFERRADA** *p.88* ■ **VILLAFRANCA DEL BIERZO** *p.89*

■ **Compostilla:** *H******Novo** © 987 424 441 N-IV. ■ **Columbrianos:** **CR Almendro De María** €50+ © 633 481 100 c/ Real 56. **San Blas** *Priv.[18÷3]*+ €8 +€30 © 611 614 149 c/ San Blas 5 (XVII). ■ **Camponaraya** *Fuentes Nuevas: [El Camino* © *672 057 061 c/ Médicos sin Fronteras, 8 + 500m].* ❶ **Naraya** *Priv.[26÷5]* €8 © 987 459 159 Av. de Galicia, 506. ❷ **La Medina** *Priv.[20÷2]* €10 © 987 463 962 m: 667 348 551 Av. Camino de Santiago, 87. ■ **CACABELOS:** *H*** **Moncloa de San Lázaro** €75 © 987 546 101 Plaza San Lázaro. *Iglesia Santa María XVI.* **Turismo** © 987 546 011. *H**** **Villa** €36 © 987 548 148. *Hs*** **Santa María** © 987 549 588 *c/Santa Maria,* 20. *Hs* **El Molino** © 987 546 829 *c/Santa Maria,*10. *Alb. Hs** **La Gallega** *Priv.[30÷7]* €10 © 987 549 476 m: 680 917 109 *c/Santa Maria,*23. *Las Angustias Alb.* **Cacabelos** *Muni.[70÷35]* © 987 547 167 Plaza del Santuario adj. *Capilla de Las Angustia XVIII.* ● +3 km **Monasterio de San Salvador de Carrecedo** *X Alb.* **Monasterio** *Priv.[20÷1]*+ €10-30 © 608 888 211 *(Begatur).* ■ **Pieros** *Alb.* **El Serbal y la Luna** *Priv.*[20÷3] V.* © 639 888 924. *CR* **Castro Ventosa** © 670 508 530 San Roque. ■ **Valtuille de Arriba: La Osa Mayor** CR © 987 562 185.

Ponferrada:_Castillo de los Templarios._

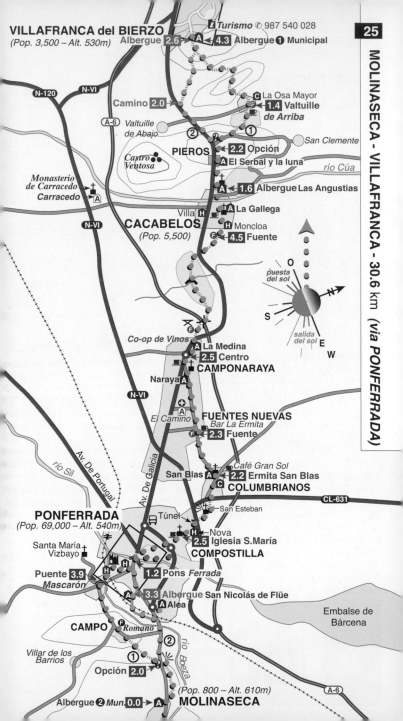

VILLAFRANCA del BIERZO
(Pop. 3,500 – Alt. 530m)

ℹ *Turismo* ℡ 987 540 028

Albergue **2.6** → A ← **4.3** Albergue ❶ Municipal

N-120   N-VI

Camino **2.0** →

A-6   Valtuille
de Abajo

C La Osa Mayor
F **1.4** Valtuille
de Arriba

② ② ①   San Clemente

PIEROS   **2.2** Opción

Castro
Ventosa   A El Serbal y la luna

río Cúa

*Monasterio
de Carracedo*   † A
Carracedo

A **1.6** Albergue Las Angustias

Villa   A La Gallega   H

CACABELOS
(Pop. 5,500)   H Moncloa
F **4.5** Fuente

N-VI

puesta
del sol

O

S   N

E
salida   W
del sol

Co-op de Vinos   ✈ †
F

A La Medina
2.5 Centro
CAMPONARAYA

Naraya A

† A
El Camino   **FUENTES NUEVAS**
Bar La Ermita
F **2.3** Fuente

N-VI

Café Gran Sol
San Blas A † **2.2** Ermita San Blas
C **COLUMBRIANOS**   CL-631

Av. De Portugal

río Sil

Av. De Galicia

† San Esteban

Túnel   † H ← Nova
2.5 Iglesia S.María
COMPOSTILLA

PONFERRADA
(Pop. 69,000 – Alt. 540m)

Santa María †
Vizbayo ■   H   H   H

Puente **3.9**   A   **1.2** Pons *Ferrada*
Mascarón

A   **3.3** Albergue San Nicolás de Flüe
A Alea

CAMPO   F *Romano*

*Villar de los
Barrios*   ②

①   *río Boeza*

Opción **2.0**

Embalse de
Bárcena

(Pop. 800 – Alt. 610m)   A-6

Albergue ❷ *Mun.* **0.0** → A **MOLINASECA**

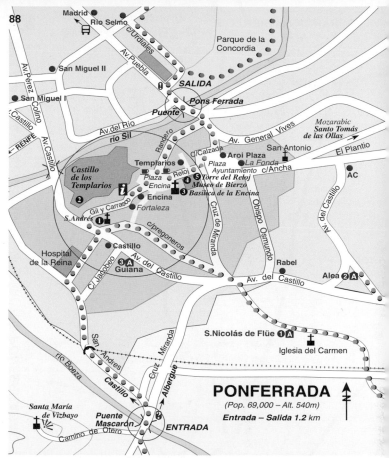

PONFERRADA *(Pop. 69,000 – Alt. 540m)*
Entrada – Salida 1.2 km

❚ **PONFERRADA:** *(pop. 69,000) Turismo:* ✆ 987 424 236 c/ Gil y carrasco, 4
Monumentos: ❶ *Iglesia San Andrés XVII (Cristo del Castillo).* ❷ *Castillo de los Templarios XII.* ❸ *Basílica de la Encina XVI* Plaza Virgen de la Encina. ❹ *Cárce* *Real XVI y Museo del Bierzo.* ❺ *La Torre del Reloj XVI.*

❚ *Albergues:* ❶ **San Nicolás de Flüe** *Par.[174÷10]* €-donativo ✆ 987 413 381 c de la Loma (Av. del Castillo). ❷ **Alea** *Priv.[18÷4]* €10 *menú* €7. ✆ 987 404 133 c Teleno, 33. ❸ **Guiana** *Priv.[90÷18]* €12 ✆ 987 409 327 (Ana) Av. del Castillo 112
❚ *Hoteles Centro:* Hs** **Rabel** €38 ✆ 987 417 176 Av del Castillo, 84. H*** **E** **Castillo** €45+ ✆ 987 456 227 Av del Castillo, 115. Hs** **Virgen de la Encina** €35 ✆

987 409 632 c/Comendador (adj. Turismo). Hs**
Los Templarios €35 ✆ 987 411 484 c/Flore
Osorío. H***Aroi Bierzo Plaza** €55+ ✆ 987 409
001 Plaza del Ayuntamiento. *Otros:* Hs* **Río**
Selmo €35 ✆ 987 402 665 c/Río Selmo,22. H**
Madrid ✆ 987 411 550 Av. Puebla,44. Hs **San**
Miguel II ✆ 987 426 700 c/Juan de Lama,18
Hs **San Miguel I** ✆ 987 411 047 c/Lucian
Fernández,2.

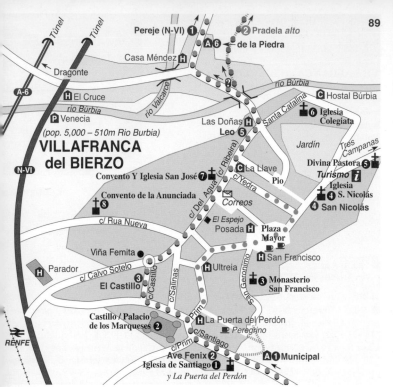

Túnel Túnel
Pereje (N-VI) ❶   ❷ Pradela *alto*
Ⓐ❻ — de la Piedra
Casa Méndez Ⓗ
Dragonte
río Búrbia
Ⓐ-6
Ⓗ El Cruce   Ⓖ Hostal Búrbia
río Búrbia   Santa Catalina
Ⓟ Venecia   ✝❻ Iglesia
Las Doñas Ⓗ   Colegiata
(pop. 5,000 – 510m Río Búrbia)   Leo ❺
VILLAFRANCA   Jardín   Tres Campanas
del BIERZO   Ⓒ La Llave   Divina Pastora ❺✝
(N-VI)   Pío   *Turismo* 🛈
Convento Y Iglesia San José ❼✝ c/Ribeira   c/Yedra   ✝ Iglesia
Convento de la Anunciada   ✉   ✝❹ S. Nicolás
✝❽   Correos   ❹ San Nicolás
c/ Rua Nueva   ◆ El Espejo
   Posada Ⓗ   Plaza
Viña Femita ●   Mayor ●
Ⓗ Parador   c/ Calvo Sotelo   Ⓗ San Francisco
❸   Ⓗ Ultreia   ✝❸ Monasterio
El Castillo   San Francisco
Castillo / Palacio   Ⓗ La Puerta del Perdón
de los Marqueses ❷   ● Peregrino
RENFE   c/Santiago
Ave Fenix ❷   Ⓐ❶ Municipal
Iglesia de Santiago ❶
y La Puerta del Perdón

▌ **VILLAFRANCA DEL BIERZO:** *(pop. 3,500) Turismo* ℂ 987 540 028 Av. Bernardo Díez Olebar. *Monumentos Históricos:* ❶ *Iglesia de Santiago XI Puerta de Perdón.* ❷ *Castillo Palacio de los Marqueses XV.* ❸ *Monasterio de San Francisco* c/San Geronimo. ❹ *Iglesia San Nicolás XVII.* ❺ *Convento Divina Pastora.* ❻ *Iglesia Colegiata (Iglesia N.S. de Cluniaco).* ❼ *Convento y Iglesia de San José XVIII.* ❽ *Convento de la Anunciada.*

▌ *Albergues:* ❶ **Municipal** *[62÷3]* €6 ℂ 987 542 356. ❷ **Ave Fenix** *Asoc.[80÷5]* €5 ℂ 987 540 229. *menú comunitarias* €7 / *Queimada.* ❸ **El Castillo** *Priv.[22÷4]* €10 ℂ 987 540 344 (Marta y Javi) c/ El Castillo 8. ❹ **San Nicolás El Real** *Priv.[75÷4]+* €5-30 ℂ 696 978 653 adj. Plaza Mayor. ❺ **Leo** *Priv.[32÷7]* €10 ℂ 987 542 658 m: 658 049 244 c/Ribadeo (c/ del Agua), 10. ❻ **de la Piedra** *Priv.*[17 ÷2]+* €10 +€24-30 ℂ 987 540 260 c/Espíritu Santo,14. *[Viña Femita Av. Calvo Sotelo 2 cerrado]*

▌ *Hoteles:* H**** **Parador** €75+ ℂ 987 540 175 Av. Calvo Sotelo. **La Puerta del Perdón** €50 ℂ 987 540 045 Plaza Prim, 4. *Adj. Plaza Mayor:* €45-55: Hs **Ultreia** ℂ 987 540 391 c/ Puentecillo. H***Posada Plaza Mayor** ℂ 987 540 620. H* **San Francisco** ℂ 987 540 465. CR **La Llave** ℂ 987 542 739 c/del Agua,37. *adj. Río:* H*** **Las Doñas del Portazgo** ℂ 987 542 742. Hs** **Burbia** ℂ 987 542 667 Fuente Cubero, 13. Hs** **Casa Méndez** ℂ 987 540 055 c/ Espíritu Santo 1. Hs* **El Cruce** ℂ 987 542 469 c/San Salvador 37. P* **Venecia** ℂ 987 540 468.

< Pradela
< Pereje

26 **185.7** km (115.4 ml) – Santiago

VILLAFRANCA del BIERZO – O'CEBREIRO

CASTILLA Y LEÓN   GALICIA

....	--- ---	15.3	--- ---	53%
————	--- ---	11.4	--- ---	39%
————	--- ---	2.2	--- ---	8%
Total km		28.9 km	(18.0 ml)	

▰▰ --- --- 33.4 km (^900m + 4.5 km)

Alto ▲ O Cebreiro 1,310m (4,297 ft).

O'CEBREIRO 1,300m

1200m
1000m — 1,050m▲ 930m — Laguna de Castilla **A** 1,150m
Dragonte ○ Alto Pradela — La Faba **A** 920m
800m — Pradela — Herrerías
600m — Portela — Valcarce **A** 705m
VILLAFRANCA ❶ Trabedelo **A** — **A** **A** **A**
500m — *Río Burbia* Pereje — *Río Valcarce*

00 km   5 km   10 km   15 km   20 km   25 km

❶ **Ruta Carretera N-VI [28.9** km]. ❷ **Ruta Pradela [30.1** km] *[Alb. Lamas Priv. [10÷1] €5 / menú €10 © 677 569 764 + 1 km Pradela].* ▮ **Pereje:** *Alb.* **Pereje** *Muni. [56÷2]* €5 © 987 540 138. *CR* **Las Corinas** © 987 540 138. ▮ **Trabadelo:** *Alb.* ❶ **Casa Susi** *Priv.[12÷2]* €-don. © 675 242 114. ❷ **Crispeta** *Priv.[34÷5]*+ €6–€25 © 620 329 386. ❸ **Parroquial** *[22÷4]* €5 © 630 628 130 c/La Iglesia. ❹ **Municipal** *[36÷6]* €6 © 687 827 987. ❺ **Camino y Leyenda** *Priv.[16÷6]*+ €8–€28 © 628 921. *CR* **El Puente Peregrino** €38 © 987 566 500. *CR* **Os Arroxos.** *CR* **Casa Ramón** © 665 610 028. *CR* **Pilar Frade** © 649 844 307. *Hs* **Nova Ruta** €50 © 987 566 431 N-VI. *Alb.* **Casa Susi** *Priv.[12÷2]* €-don. ▮ **Portela:** *H**** **Valcarce** €25 © 987 543 180 N-VI. ▮ **La Portela de Valcarce:** *Hs* + Alb.* ❶ **El Peregrino** *Priv.[28÷8]*+ €9–€25 © 987 543 197. *Hs+ Alb* ❷ **Camynos** *Priv.[10÷1]*+ €10–€35 © 609 381 412 ▮ **Ambasmestas:** *Alb.* ❶ **Casa Del Pescador** *Priv.[10÷2]* €10-12 +€45 © 603 515 868. ❷ **Das Animas** *Priv.[18÷1]* €5 © 619 048 626 c/Campo Bajo. ❸ **El Rincón del Apóstol** €19 +€40 © 987 543 099. *CR* **Ambasmestas** © 987 233 768 €30+ ▮ **VEGA DE VALCARCE:** *Antigua N-VI:* *CR* **El Recanto** © 987 543 202. ❶ **Sarracin** *Priv.[14÷1]* €10 © 696 982 672 adj. río +*CR* **Panaderia.** *Centro:* ❷ **Santa María Magdalena** *Priv.[8÷1]*+ €8 +€26 © 987 543 230. *CR* **Meson Las Rocas** © 987 543 208. ❸ **Municipal.** *[92÷7]* €5 © 722 786 186 c/Pandelo. *CR* **Pandelo** © 987 543 033. ❹ **Isana** *V. Priv.[12÷4]*+ €5 © 617 056 179 Menú *macrobiotica* €9. ❺ **El Paso** *Priv.[28÷6]*+ €10 © 628 104 309 (Lalo) adj. church. *Over río:* ❻ *P* **Fernández** €15+ © 987 543 027 Plaza del Ayuntamiento. ❼ **Virgen de la Encina** *Par.[26÷5,* €-donativo © 649 133 272. ▮ **Ruitelán:** *Alb.* **Pequeño Potala** *Priv.[34÷3]*+ €5–€30 © 987 561 322. *CR* **El Paraíso del Bierzo** €40 © 987 684 137. *CR* **El Capricho de Josana** €32 © 987 119 300. ▮ **Herrerías:** *Alb.* ❶ **Las Herrerías** *Priv.[17÷2]* V © 654 353 940. *Alb.* ❷ **Casa Lixa** *Priv.[15÷2]*+ €12+€45/59 © 987 134 915. *CR* **A Casa do Ferreiro** © 987 684 903. *CR* **Polín** €30 © 987 543 039. ▮ **La Faba** *Alb.* **La Faba** *Asoc.[66÷3]* © 630 836 865. **Laguna de Castilla:** *Alb.* **La Faba** *Priv.*[20÷3]* © 987-684 786. ▮ **O'CEBREIRO** *Iglesia de Santa Maria Real X* (*Santo Milagro*). *Don Elias Valiña Sampedro* → (1929–1989). *Alb.* **O'Cebreiro** *Xunta.* *[104÷3]* €6 © 660 396 809. *H* **O Cebreiro** © 982 367 182. **San Giraldo de Aurillac** © 982 367 125. *CR* **Casa Carolo** © 982 367 168. *CR* **Venta Celta** © 66? 553 006. *CR* **Casa valiña** © 982 367 182. *CR* **Casa Frade** © 982 367 104.

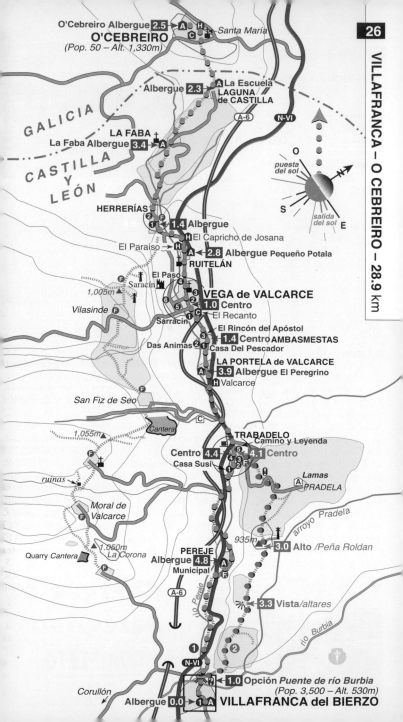

O'Cebreiro Albergue **2.5** A H *Santa María*
O'CEBREIRO C
(Pop. 50 – Alt. 1,330m)

GALICIA

Albergue **2.3** A La Escuela
LAGUNA de CASTILLA
A-6 N-VI

CASTILLA

LA FABA †
La Faba Albergue **3.4** A

Y

LEÓN

HERRERÍAS
1.4 Albergue
H El Capricho de Josana
El Paraíso H A **2.8** Albergue *Pequeño Potala*
RUITELÁN
El Paso
1,005m Saracín F
VEGA de VALCARCE
Vilasinde F **1.0** Centro
C El Recanto
Sarracín El Rincón del Apóstol
1.4 Centro **AMBASMESTAS**
Das Ánimas Casa Del Pescador
LA PORTELA de VALCARCE
A **3.9** Albergue El Peregrino
H Valcarce

San Fiz de Seo F

1,055m Cantera C
TRABADELO
Camino y Leyenda
Centro **4.4** **4.1** Centro
Casa Susi *Lamas*
A **PRADELA**
arroyo Pradela
Moral de Valcarce F
Quarry *Cantera* *1,050m* La Corona
935m **3.0** Alto /*Peña Roldán*
F
PEREJE
Albergue **4.8** A
Municipal F
A-6 **3.3** Vista/*altares*

río Pereje

río Burbia

1
N-VI
1.0 Opción *Puente de río Burbia*
(Pop. 3,500 – Alt. 530m)
Corullón
Albergue **0.0** A **VILLAFRANCA del BIERZO**

puesta
del sol
O

S
salida
del sol
E

27　**156.8** km (97.4 ml) – Santiago

O'CEBREIRO – TRIACASTELA

....	--- ---	19.7 --- ---	95%
	--- ---	1.0 --- ---	05%
▬▬	--- ---	0.0	
Total km		**20.7** km (12.9 ml)	

▲▲ --- --- 21.7 km (+1.0 km)

Alto ▲ Alto do Poio 1,335m (4,380 ft)

< **Ⓐ Ⓗ** > Liñares **3.1** km – Hospital **5.6** km – Alto do Poio **8.6** km – Fonfría **11.9** km – Biduedo **14.3** km – Filloval **17.4** km.

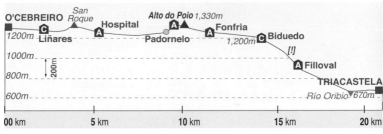

❚ **Liñares: Linar do Rei** *Priv.[22÷4]*+ €10+ €40 ✆ 616 464 831 (Erica). *CR* **Casa Jaime** ✆ 982 367 166. ❚ **Hospital de la Condesa:** *Alb.* **Xunta.***[20÷1]* €6 ✆ 660 396 810. *CR* **O Tear** ✆ 982 367 183. ❚ **Alto do Poio:** *Alb.* **del Puerto** *Priv.* *[16÷1]* €6 ✆ 982 367 172. *Hs* **Santa María de Poio** ✆ 982 367 167. ❚ **Fonfría:** *CR* **Núñez** ✆ 982 161 335. *CR* **Galego** €25-35 ✆ 982 161 461. *Alb.* **A Reboleira** *Priv.*[64÷3]*+ €8 ✆ 982 181 271. ❚ **Biduedo**: *CR* **Quiroga** CR ✆ 982 187 299. *CR* **Xata** ✆ 982 187 301. ■ **Filloval:** *Alb.* **Filloval** *Priv.[18÷2]*+ €9–€30 ✆ 666 826 414. ❚ **TRIACASTELA:** *Albergue* ❶ Xunta.*[56÷14]* €6. *P°* **García** ✆ 982 548 024. *Alb* ❷ **Lemos** *Priv.[12÷1]*+ €9 + €40 ✆ 677 117 238. ❸ **Oribio** *Priv.[27÷2]* €8 ✆ 982 548 085. *C/del Peregrino:* ❹ **A Horta de Abel** *Priv.[14÷2]*+ €9–€40 ✆ 608 080 556. *P°* **Fernandez** ✆ 982 548 148. *P°* **Casa Simón** adj. *Igrexa de Santiago (misa del peregrino 18:00).* ❺ **Atrio** *Priv.[20÷4]*+ €9 +€40-50 ✆ 982 548 488 (Juan José). ❻ **Complexo Xacobeo** *Priv*.[36÷3]*+ €9–€40 ✆ 982 548 037 adj. *Bar-rst. Xacobeo. Hs* **O'Novo** ✆ 982 548 105. ❼ **Aitzenea** *Priv.[38÷4]*+ €8 ✆ 982 548 076. ❽ **Berce do Camiño** *Priv.[27÷6]* €8 ✆ 982 548 127. *P°°* **Casa David** ✆ 982 548 105. **Mesón Vilasante** €30-40 ✆ 982 548 116. *CR* **Olga** €16+ p.p ✆ 982 548 134 c/ Castro 2 (+0.5 km). *CR* **Pacios** €35+ ✆ 982 548 455 Vilavella (+ 2.0 km) transporte desde rst. Esther Rúa Peregrino.

Triacastela: *Xunta albergue*

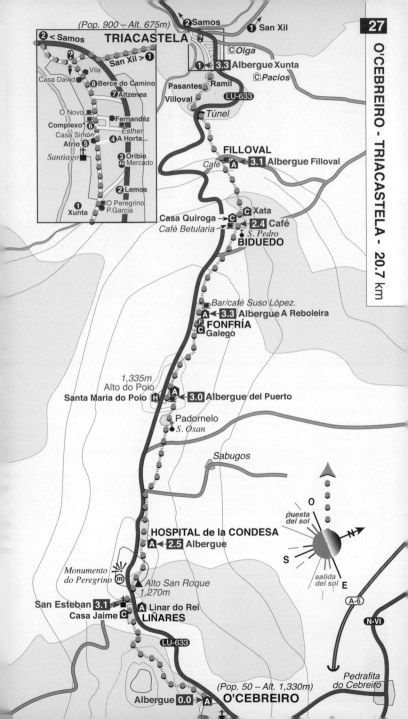

(Pop. 900 – Alt. 675m)
2 < Samos **TRIACASTELA**

2 Samos   **1** San Xil

ⓒ *Olga*

1 **3.3** Albergue Xunta

ⓒ *Pacios*

San Xil > **1**
† Vila
Casa Dawd
8 Berce do Camino
7 Aitzenea
O Novo
Complexo* **6**
Fernández
Esther
Casa Simón
Atrio **5** **4** A Horta...
Santiago **†**
3 Oribio
Ⓜ Mercado
2 Lemos
1 O Peregrino
Xunta   P.Garcia

Pasantes   Ramil
Villoval   Pantes
       LU-633
Túnel

FILLOVAL
Café Ⓐ **3.1** Albergue Filloval

Casa Quiroga →ⓒ ‖ ⓒ Xata
Café Betularia →▪‖Ⓐ **2.4** Café
        ▪ *S. Pedro*
     BIDUEDO

Bar/café Suso López.
Ⓐ◄ **3.3** Albergue A Reboleira
Ⓕ
FONFRÍA
ⓒ
Galego

1,335m
Alto do Poio
Santa Maria do Poio Ⓗ‖Ⓐ **3.0** Albergue del Puerto

Ⓜ Padornelo
   † *S. Oxan*

Sabugos

HOSPITAL de la CONDESA
Ⓐ◄ **2.5** Albergue

Monumento
do Peregrino Ⓜ
      ▲ *Alto San Roque*
        1,270m
San Esteban **3.1** **†**
Casa Jaime ⓒ‖Ⓐ Linar do Rei
     LIÑARES
       LU-633

(Pop. 50 – Alt. 1,330m)
Albergue **0.0** ►Ⓐ **O'CEBREIRO**
         †

O
puesta del sol
S
salida del sol E

Ⓐ-6

N-VI

Pedrafita do Cebreiro

28 **136.1** km (84.6 ml) – Santiago

TRIACASTELA – SARRIA (via San Xil)

.... --- ---	11.2 --- ---	*60%*
▬▬▬ --- ---	7.5 --- ---	*40%*
▬▬▬ --- ---	0.0	
Total km	**18.7** km (11.6 ml)	

◣ --- --- 20.1 km (+ 1.4 km)
Alto ▲ Alto do Riocabo 905m (2,970 ft)
< 🅰 🏠 > ❶ *San Xil:* A Balsa **1.6** km –
Pintín **12.1** km– Calvor **13.4** km
San Mamed **14.8** km – Vigo de Sarria **17.7** km.
❷ *Samos:* Lusío **5.1** km (+ 0.4) – Samos **10.5** km –San Mamed **21.4** km

❶ ● ▌ **A Balsa:** *Alb.* **El Beso** *Priv.[12÷1]* V. €8 ℂ 633 550 558. **Montán** *[Tierra de la Luz]*. **Fontearcuda** *Casa Campo. [Mondaviega Alquimista].*▌ **Pintín:** *P°* **Casa Cines** ℂ 982 167 939. ▌ **Calvor:** *Alb.* **Calvor** *Xunta.[22÷2]* €6 ℂ 660 396 812.

❷ ● /● *Lusío* + 400m: *Alb.* **Casa Grande** *Xunta.[60÷4]* €6 *(Monasterio de Samos)*. ▌**SAMOS:** *Alb.* ❶ **Val de Samos** *Priv.[48÷7]* €9 ℂ 982 546 163. ❷ **Monasterio de Samos** *Conv.[70÷1]* €-donativo *(misa del peregrino 19:30 turismo: 09:30-18:30)*. *Capilla Ciprés S.Salvador IX!* ❸ **Albaroque** *Priv.[6÷1]*+ €9–€25 ℂ 982 546 087 / 628 828 845. ❹ **Casa Licerio** *Priv.[20÷3]*+ €15–€30/40 ℂ 653 593 814. *HsR°* **Victoria** ℂ 982 546 022. *HsR°* **Domus Itineris** ℂ 982 546 088. *Hs°* **A Veiga** ℂ 982 546 052. *CR* **Casas Outeiro** spa €75+ ℂ 680 379 969 c/ Fontao.

▌ **S. Mamed del Camino:** *Alb.* **Paloma y Leña** *Priv.*[20÷3]+ €10–€40 ℂ 982 533 248. **Camping Vila de Sarria** *[12÷1]*+ €6 ℂ 982 535 467. *P°* **Ana** ℂ 982 531 458. ▌ **VIGO DE SARRIA:** (albergues ±€10) *Alb.*● **A Pedra** *Priv.*[14÷3]+ ℂ 982 530 130. *Turismo* ℂ 982 530 099 adj. *Alb.*● **Oasis** *Priv.[27÷4]* ℂ 605 948 644. *Hs* **Cristal** ℂ 669 799 512. *Alb.*● **Alma do Camiño** *Priv.[96÷10]* ℂ 982 876 768 c/ Calvo Sotclo, 199. ■ **SARRIA** *Centro:* *p.97*

Samos:

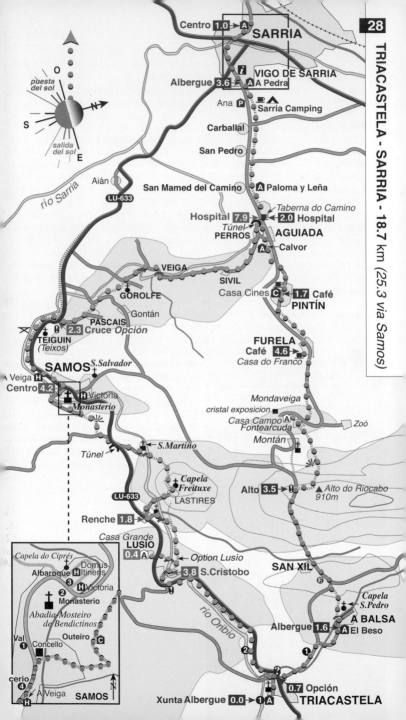

▮ SARRIA: (albergues ±€10) *Alb.*● **Barullo** *Café* ℂ 982 876 357 Praza de Galicia. **Rúa do Peregrino Bajo Nº44** *Alb.*● **Credencial** *Priv.[96÷10]* ℂ 982 876 455. **Nº23** *Alb.*● **Puente Ribeira** *Priv.[40÷4]* ℂ 982 876 789. *H***** **Alfonso IX** €85 ℂ 982 530 005. *H*** **Oca Villa** €45 ℂ 982 533 873 c/Benigno Quiroga. *P* **O Camiño** €40+ ℂ 626 205 172. •*Peregrinoteca (trekking)* ℂ 982 530 190 Escalinata Maior.

▮ Sarria *Centro [km. 111,5] rúa Maior.* **Albergues ❶ – ❾** (± €10). ❶ **Casa Peltre** *Priv [22÷3]* ℂ 606 226 067 Escalinata da Fonte. *P** **Escalinata** €20 ℂ 982 530 259. *Rúa Maior:* **Nº64 ❷ Mayor** *Priv.[16÷2]* ℂ 646 427 734. **Nº79 ❸ Xunta.***[40÷2]* ℂ 660 396 813 (€6). **Nº62** *H* **Aqua** €35 ℂ 619 879 476. **Nº44 ❹ O Durmiñento** *Priv.[40÷7]+* ℂ 982 531 099. **Nº65 ❺ Casino** *Priv [28÷2]* ℂ 982 886 785. **Nº53 Casa Barán** €75 ℂ 982 876 487. **Nº57 ❻ Internacional** *Priv.[44÷4]+* ℂ 982 535 109. **Nº49 ❼ Obradoiro** *Priv.[28÷2]* ℂ 982 532 442. **Nº31 ❽ Los Blasones** *Priv.*[42÷4]* ℂ 600 512 565. *Mesón O Tapas.* **Nº10 ❾ Don Álvaro** *Priv.[40÷4]* ℂ 982 531 592. **Nº4 ❿ Matías** *Priv.[30÷1]+* ℂ 982 534 285 rest' Matias Locanda Italiana. ● Otros albergues: ● **Dos Oito Marabedís** *Priv.[24÷7]* ℂ 629 461 770 rúa Conde de Lemos, 23. ● **Barbacoa** *Priv.[10÷1]+* ℂ 619 879 476 c/Esqueirodos,1. ● **San Lázaro** *Priv.[30÷4]+* ℂ 982 530 626 c/San Lázaro,7. ● **La Casona de Sarria** *Priv.[31÷5]/+* +€35 ℂ 982 535 556 Rúa San Lázaro 24. ● **Monasterio la Magdalena** *Priv.[90÷3]* Av. de la Merced, ℂ 982 533 568.

▮ *Hostales:* *P* **Matias Rooms** €25-40 Calle Rosalia de Castro, 19 *(Alb. Matias ℂ982 534 285)*. *P** **Casa Matías** €25 ℂ 659 160 498 Calvo Sotelo,39. *H** **Mar de Plata** ℂ 982 530 724 rúa Formigueiros. *Hr** **Roma** ℂ 982 532 211 Calvo Sotelo, 2 *(adj.*

estación de tren).
Monumentos Históricos: ❶ *Iglesia de Santa Mariña XIX (credenciales y misa del peregrino 18:00).* ❷ *Iglesia del Salvador XIII.* ❸ *Hospital de San Anton XVI (antiguo hospital de peregrino).* ❹ *Fortaleza de Sarria y Torres XIII (ruinas).* ❺ *Mosteiro de Santa María Madalena XIII (Convento de la Merced. Credenciales y misa del peregrino 18:30).*

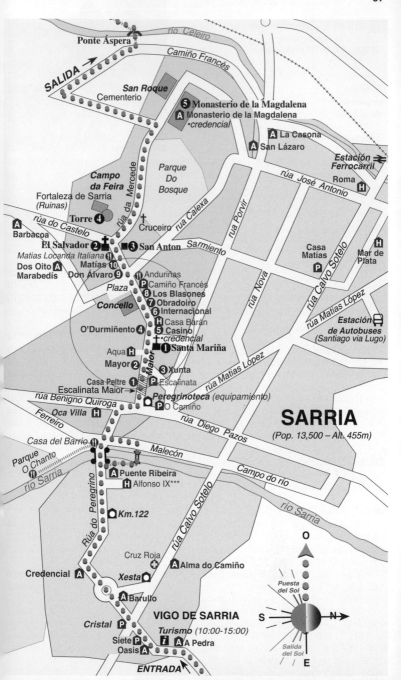

29 117.4 km (72.9 ml) – Santiago

SARRIA – PORTOMARÍN

⁞⁞⁞⁞⁞⁞⁞⁞⁞	--- ---	11.4 --- ---	*50%*
▬▬▬	--- ---	10.7 --- ---	*48%*
	--- ---	0.6 --- ---	*2%*
Total km		**22.7** km (14.1 ml)	

(^940m + 4.7 km = **27.4** km)

Alto Alto Momientos 660m (2,165 ft)

<**⌂ ⒣**> Barbadelo **❶ 3.7 – ❺ 4.5** km. Morgade **12.4** km. Ferrerios **13.8** km. Mercadoiro **17.3** km. Vilacha **20.4** km.

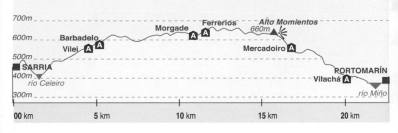

■ **Barbadelo** *Vilei: Albergue* ❶ **Casa Barbadelo** *Priv.[68÷12]*+ €9-12 ☏ 982 531 934. ❷ **108 km** *Priv.[12÷5]*+ €8-29 ☏ 634 894 524. ❸**O Pombal** *Priv.[12÷1]* €9 ☏ 686 718 732 (+200m). *Igrexa de Santiago XII (misa del pergrino 19:00).* ❹ **Barbadelo** *Xunta.[18÷2]* €6. ❺ **Casa de Carmen** *Priv.[26÷3]*+ €9-35 ☏ 982 532 294 *Capela de San Silvestre (privado).* ■ **Rente:** *CR* **Casa Nova** ☏ 982 187 854. / *Alb.* **Granxa de Barreiros** *Priv.[46÷8]*+ €10 +18 ☏ 982 533 656 *Ortoá LU-633).* ■**Peruscallo:** *Alb.* **Molino de Marzán** *Priv.[16÷1]* €10 ☏ 679 438 077. ■ **Morgade** *Alb.* **Casa Morgade** *Priv.[6÷1]*+ €10-28 ☏ 982 531 250. ■ **Ferreiros:** *Alb.* ❶ **Casa Cruceiro** *Priv.[12÷1]*+ €10-40 ☏ 982 541 240. ❷ **Ferreiros** *Xunta.[22÷1]* €6 ☏ 686 744 940. ■ **A Pena:** *Alb.* **Casa do Rego** *Priv.[6÷1]*+ €10 ☏ 982 167 812. ■**Mercadoiro:** *Alb.* **Mercadoiro** *& café Bodeguiña Priv.[32÷6]*+ €10-40 ☏ 982 545 359. ■ **Vilachá:** *Alb.* **Casa Banderas** *Priv.[8÷1]*+ €10-40 ☏ 982 545 391. ■*Fontedeagra* +0.5km Alb. **A Fontana de Luxo** €15+35 ☏ 645 649 496.

PORTOMARÍN: (albergues Av. €10) ❶ **Pons Minea** *Priv.[12÷1]*+ ☏ 610 737 995 Av. Sarria (bajo). ❷ **O Mirador** *Priv.[27÷6]* ☏ 982 545 323 *bar/rest'* adj' ❸ **Ferrameteiro** *Priv.*[130÷1]* ☏ 982 545 362. ❹ **Folgueira** *Priv.[32÷1]* ☏ 982 545 166 Av. Chantada opp' *H**Ferrameteiro* €80 ☏ 982 545 361. ❺ **Pasiño a Pasiño** *Priv.[30÷6]* ☏ 665 667 243 Rúa Compostela 25. ❻ **Villamartín** *Priv.[20÷2]* ☏ 982 545 054 rúa Miño. c/ *Benigno Quiroga* Nº16 ❼ **Casa Cruz** *Priv.[16÷1]* ☏ 982 545 140. Nº12 ❽ **Novo Porto** *Priv.[22÷1]* ☏ 982 545 277. Nº6 ❾ **El Caminante** *Priv.[12÷1]*+ ☏ 982 545 176. *c/ Diputación* Nº9 ●10 **Ultreia** *Priv.[14÷1]*+ ☏ 982 545 067 opp. Nº8 ●11 **Porto Santiago** *Priv.*[14÷1]*+ ☏ 618 826 515. ●12 **Aqua** *Priv.[16÷1]*+ ☏ 608 921 372 Barreiros, 2. ●13 **Portomarín** *Xunta.[110÷6]* (€6) ☏ 982 545 143. ●14 **Manuel** *Priv.[16÷1]*+ ☏ 982 545 385. ●15 **Casa do Marabillas** *Priv.[20÷2]* ☏ 982 189 086 Camiño do Monte 3.■ *Hostales:* *P'* **Posada del Camino** ☏ 982 545 081. *P**Arenas* ☏ 982 545 386. *H** **Villajardín** ☏ 982 545 054 rúa Miño,14. *H*** **Pousada de Portomarín** ☏ 982 545 200.

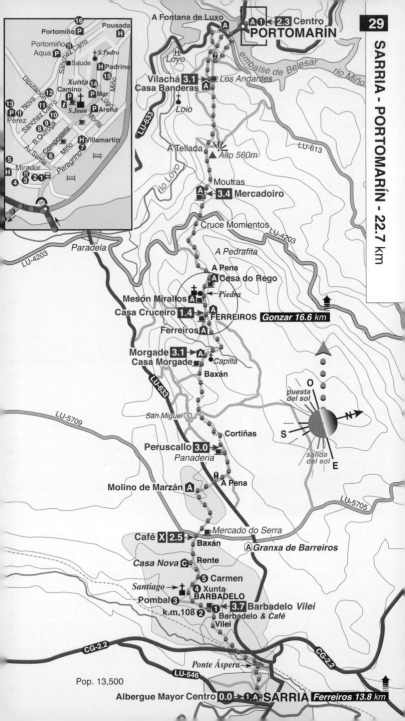

A Fontana de Luxo

A 🅰**1** ← **2.3** Centro
PORTOMARÍN

Portomiño **P**
H Pousada
Portomiño
Aqua **P**
Saude **H** Padrino **15**
Xunta **14**
Camino **H** Mar
12 **S.Juan** Arena
13
Perez **11** **10**
8 B.Quiroga
5 **6** Compostela
H Villamartín **H**
Mirador **7**
4 **3** **2** **1**

S.Pedro

Loyo **H**

embalse de Belesar   rio Miño

Vilachá **3.1**
Casa Banderas **A** ● Los Andantes
Loio

LU-633

A Tellada ⚡ 🔺 Alto 560m   LU-613

Moutras

A ● **3.4** Mercadoiro

Paradela

Cruce Momientos   LU-4203

LU-4203

A Pedrafita

A Pena
A Casa do Rego
● ← Piedra
Mesón Mirallos **A**
Casa Cruceiro **1.4** **A** **FERREIROS** *Gonzar 16.6 km*
Ferreiros **A**

Morgade **3.1** **A**
Casa Morgade ● ← *Capilla*
Baxán

LU-633

San Miguel ☐

puesta
del sol

O

Cortiñas

Peruscallo **3.0** →
Panaderia

S

N

LU-5709

🔺

θ A Pena
Molino de Marzán **A**

salida
del sol

E

LU-5705

Mercado do Serra

Café **X** **2.5**
Baxán
A *Granxa de Barreiros*

Casa Nova **C**
Rente

5 Carmen
Santiago → ✝ **4** Xunta
Pombal **3** **BARBADELO**
k.m.108 **2** **1** ← **3.7** Barbadelo *Vilei*
Barbadelo & *Café*
Vilei

CG-2.2

CG-2.2

Ponte Áspera →
LU-546

Pop. 13,500

30 **94.7** km (58.8 ml) – Santiago

PORTOMARÍN – PALAS DE REI

,,,,,,,,,,,,,,,,,,	--- ---	19.8	--- ---	*80%*
▬▬▬	--- ---	4.8	--- ---	*20%*
▬▬▬	--- ---	0.0		
Total km	**24.6** km	(15.3 ml)		

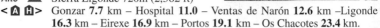

▲ (^1,050m + 5.2 km = **29.8** km)

Alto ▲ Sierra Ligonde 720m (2,362 ft)

< Ⓐ Ⓗ > Gonzar **7.7** km – Hospital **11.0** – Ventas de Narón **12.6** km –Ligonde **16.3** km – Eirexe **16.9** km – Portos **19.1** km – Os Chacotes **23.4** km.

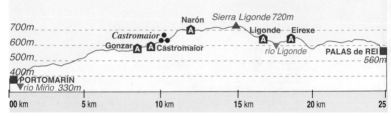

■ **Gonzar:** *Alb.* ❶ Gonzar *Xunta.[28÷1]* €6. *Alb.* ❷ Casa Garcia *Priv.[30÷5]*+ €10–€35 ✆ 982 157 842 (+100m). ■ **Castromaior** *P* ` *Casa Maruja* ✆ 982 189 054. ■ **Hospital de la Cruz:** *Hs* El Labrador €30+ ✆ 982 545 303. *Alb.* **Hospital de la**

Cruz *Xunta.[32÷1]* €6. ■ **Ventas de Narón:** *Alb.* ❶ Casa Molar *Priv.[18÷2]*+ €10-30 ✆ 696 794 507. *Alb.* ❷ O Cruceiro *Priv.*[22÷2]*+ €10-30 ✆ 658 064 917.■ **Ligonde:** *Alb.*❶ Fuente del Peregrino *Priv.[20÷2]* €-donativo ✆ 687 550 527. ❷ Escuela de Ligonde *Muni.[20]* ✆ 679 816 061. ■ **Eirexe:** *Alb.* ❶ Airexe *Xunta.[20÷2]* €6. ❷ Eirexe *Priv.[6÷1]*+ €10 ✆ 982 153 475. *Cruceiro XVII.* ■ **Portos:** *Alb.* A Paso de Formiga *Priv.[8÷1]*+ €10– €25 ✆ 618 984 605. ■ **Portos** *A Calzada*: *Alb.* A Calzada *Priv.[10÷1]* €10 ✆ 982 183 744. ● *Vilar de Donas: (+2.3 km x2).* ■ **Lestedo:** *CR* Rectoral de Lestedo €60+ ✆ 982 153 435.

■ **PALAS de REI** *Parque:* *Alb.* ❶ Os Chacotes *Xunta.[112÷3]* €6 *Pavillón.* *H* `***` **Complejo La Cabana** €35+ ✆ 982 380 750. *Centro:* (albergues Av. €10) ❷ Mesón de Benito *Priv.[100÷7]* ✆ 982 103 386. ❸ Zendoira *Priv.[50÷4]*+ €10-€35 ✆ 608 490 075 (Av.Ourense). Rua Cruceiro *Hs* O Castelo ✆ 618 401 130 & *P* O Cruceiro ✆ 649 629 725. ❹ Outeiro *Priv.[50÷6]* ✆ 982 380 242 (Plaza de Galicia). Av. Ourense ❺ San Marcos *Priv.[58÷7]*+ ✆ 982 380 711 adj. *P* ` Casa Curro ✆ 982 380 044. ❻ Castro *Priv.*[56÷6]* ✆ 609 080 655. Rua Mercado *Hr* `**` Benilde ✆ 982 380 717 adj. *P* Pardellas ✆ 982 380 181. *Av.Compostela* Nº19 ❼ Xunta *[60÷7]* €6 opp. *Casa Concello.* Nº16 *P* `**`Arenas Palas ✆ 982 380 326. Nº21 *P* Hostal Plaza ✆ 982 380 109 Nº39 *P* Barcelona ✆ 982 374 114. Travesía del Peregrino (praza Concello): ❽ Buen Camino *Priv.*[41÷8]* ✆ 982 380 233 opp'. *P* ` Guntina ✆ 982 380 080 & *P* Casa Camiño *Pulpería* ✆ 982 374 066. ❾ A Casina di Marcello *Priv. [16÷2]* ✆ 640 723 903 c/Camiño de abaixo.. ■ *Turismo (Oficina Municipal)* Av. de Compostela 28 ✆ 982 380 001. *Iglesia San Tirso XII / Santiago de Alba.*

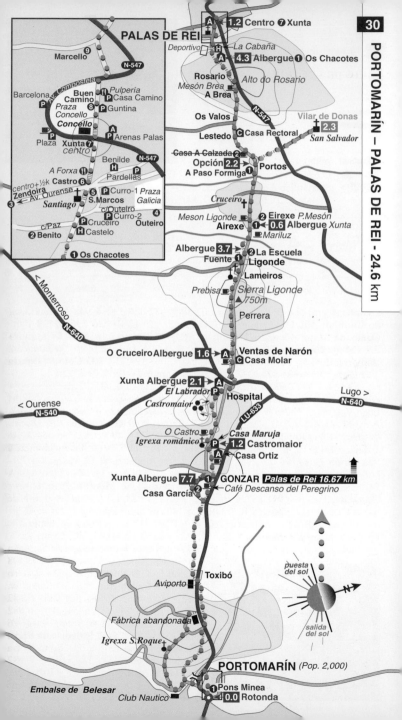

31 **70.1** km (43.6 ml) – Santiago

PALAS DE REI – RIBADISO (ARZÚA)

⁙⁙⁙⁙⁙	--- ---	18.2	--- ---	*71%*
▬▬▬	--- ---	6.6	--- ---	*26%*
▬▬▬	--- ---	0.8	--- ---	*3%*
Total km		**26.3** km	(16.3 ml)	

(^820m + 4.3 km = **30.6** km)
Alto ▲ O Coto 515m (1,670 ft)
< **A** **H** > San Xulián **3.6** km – Casanova **5.9** km – O Coto **8.7** km –
Melide **15.1** km – Boente **21.0** km – Castañeda **23.2** km.

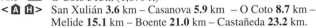

❚ Ponterroxan: N-547 *P* Ponterroxan €38 ℭ 982 380 132. **❚ San Xulián (***Xiao***)
do Camiño:** *Alb.* O Abrigadoiro *Priv.[18÷3]* €10-12 ℭ 676 596 975. **❚ Ponte
Campaña-Mato:** *Alb.* Casa Domingo *Priv.*[16÷3]* ℭ 982 163 226. **❚ Casanova:**
Alb. Mato Casanova *Xunta.[20÷2]* €6. ● *(+1½ km) Vilar de Remonde:* A
Bolboreta *Priv.[8÷2]*+ €13 incl. + €27–€37 ℭ 609 124 717. **❚ O Coto** *P*** Los dos
Alemanes €30 ℭ 981 507 337. *CR* Casa de Somoza ℭ 981 507 372.

❚ MELIDE: *Pop.7,500 Turismo* (9:00-15:00) Casa Concello Plaza Convento ℭ
981 505 003. (albergues *Av. €10)* *Alb.* ❶ Melide *Priv.[42÷2]* ℭ 627 901 552 Av.
Lugo. *Iglesia S. Pedro & S. Roque Crucero do Melide XIV. Centro:* ❷ Arraigos
Priv.[24÷1] ℭ 646 343 370 Cantón de S. Roque, 9. ❸ O Cruceiro *Priv.[72÷12]*
ℭ 616 764 896 Ronda Coruña. ❹ Alfonso II *Priv.[34÷5]* ℭ 981 506 454 Av. de
Toques y Friol 52. ❺ Vilela *Priv.[24÷2]*+ ℭ 616 011 375 c/ San Antonio, 2. ❻
San Antón *Priv.[36÷5]* ℭ 981 506 427 c/ San Antón, 6. ❼ O Apalpador *Priv.
[30÷3]* ℭ 679 837 969 c/ San Antonio, 23. ❽ Melide *Xunta.[156÷7]* (€6). *Alb* ❾
Pereiro *Priv.[45÷4]* ℭ 981 506 314 c/Progreso, 43. ❿ Montoto *Priv.[42÷2]* r/
Codeseira, 31ℭ 646 941 887. **❚ *Hoteles:*** *(Pensions €25-35)* *H***Carlos ℭ 981 507
633 Av. Lugo. *Hs***Xaneiro II ℭ 981 506 140 Av. de la Habana. *P** Orois ℭ 981
506 140 rua A.Bóvena. *P**Berenguela ℭ 981 505 417 rua S.Roque. *P**Estilo c/del
Progreso. *Pousada* Chiquitín ℭ 981 815 533 Rúa San António, 18. *H* Sony ℭ 981

505 473 N-547. **❚ Boente *Igrexa Santiago*:**
Alb. ❶ Os Albergues *Priv.[28÷7]* €11 ℭ
981 501 853. ❷ Boente *Priv.[22÷5]* ℭ 981
501 974. **❚ Castañeda:** *Alb.* Santiago *Priv.
[4÷1]*+ €10 +€35 ℭ 981 501 711. *CR* La
Calleja ℭ 605 787 382 €25+. ● *(+400m /
N-547) CR Garea* €35-40 ℭ 981 500 400 +
Milía ℭ 981 515 241. **❚ Ribadiso da Baixo:**
Alb. ❶ Ribadiso *Xunta.[70÷3]* €6. ❷ Los
Caminantes *Priv.[52÷3]*+ €10-38 ℭ 647
020 600. ❸ Milpes *Priv.[38÷3]* €10 ℭ 981
500 425. ● *(+500m / N-547) CR Vaamonde*
ℭ 981 500 364 Traseirexe.

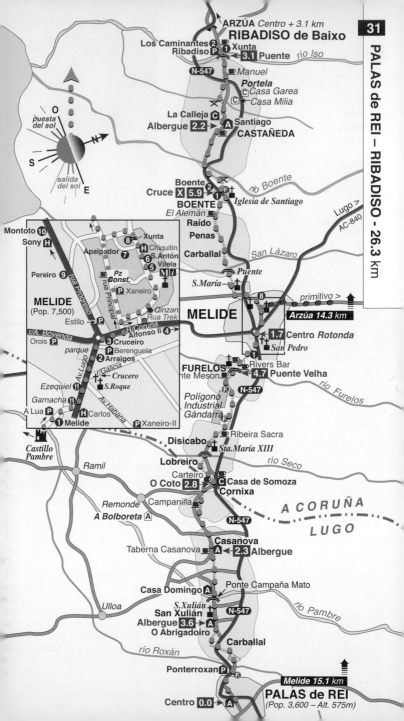

ARZÚA *Centro* + 3.1 km
RIBADISO de Baixo
Los Caminantes 2
Ribadiso P 1 Xunta
3.1 Puente   *río Iso*
N-547
Manuel
Portela
C *Casa Garea*
C *Casa Milia*
La Calleja C
Albergue 2.2   A Santiago
CASTAÑEDA

Boente 2
Cruce X 5.9
BOENTE   *Iglesia de Santiago*
El Alemán
Raído
Penas   San Lázaro
Carballal

Lugo >
AC-840

Puente
S.María→   †
8
MELIDE   Arzúa 14.3 km
primitivo >
1.7 Centro *Rotonda*
†† *San Pedro*
FURELOS   Rivers Bar
nte Meson   4.7 Puente Velha
F   N-547

*Polígono
Industrial
Gándarra*

Ribeira Sacra
Disicabo   † *Sta.María XIII*
Lobreiro   *río Seco*
Carteiro
O Coto 2.8   C Casa de Somoza
Cornixa

A CORUÑA

LUGO

Remonde
Campanilla
A Bolboreta A
N-547

Casanova
Taberna Casanova A   2.3 Albergue

Casa Domingo A   *Ponte Campaña Mato*
S.Xulián
San Xulián   N-547
Albergue 3.6 → A
O Abrigadoiro
Carballal
río Roxán

Ponterroxan P
F   **Melide 15.1 km**
Centro 0.0 → A   **PALAS de REI**
(Pop. 3,600 – Alt. 575m)

O
*puesta
del sol*
N
S
E
*salida
del sol*

Montoto 10
Sony H
Pereiro 9

MELIDE
(Pop. 7,500)

rúa progreso

Xunta 8
Apalpador   Chiquitin H
7   S.Antón 6
Vilela 5
Pz
Const.   M i
P Xaneiro
Qinzan
Rúa Trek
Estilo →   P
Alfonso II 4
t/A. Bovenda   R/Coruña
Orois P   3 Cruceiro
parque   Berenguela P
2 Arraigos
†† *Crucero*
R/Galicia   *S.Roque*
Ezequiel (1)
Garnacha (1)
A Lua P   H Carlos
1 Melide   P Xaneiro-II
Av.Habana

*Castillo
Pambre*

Ramil
Ulloa
río Pambre

32 **43.8** km (27.2 ml) – Santiago

RIBADISO – PEDROUZO *(ARCA / O PINO)*

‖‖‖‖‖‖	--- ---	12.2	--- ---	54%
	--- ---	8.2	--- ---	36%
▬▬▬	--- ---	2.4	--- ---	10%
Total km		**23.7** km (14.7 ml)		

(^1,150m + 5.7 km = **29.4** km)

Alto ▲ Santa Irene 420m (1,378 ft)

<**Ⓐ Ⓗ**> Arzúa **3.1** km – Salceda **14.1** – Santa Irene **20.0** km – A Rua **21.7** km.

■ **ARZUA:** *Pr*** Retiro €48 © 981 500 554 *Av. de Lugo* & 9 *Albergues (Av. €10).*
Albergue ❶ de Selmo *Priv.[50÷1]* © 981 939 018. *P*** Rua © 981 500 139. ❷
Santiago Apostol *Priv.[72÷3]* © 981 508 132. ❸ Don Quijote *Priv.*[50÷1]* ©
981 500 139. ❹ Ultreia *Priv.*[38÷2]* © 981 500 471. ❺ de Camino *Priv.[46÷4]+*
© 981 500 415. *Turismo* Praza do Peregrino © 981 508 056. *P*** Teodora © 981
500 083. *Iglesia de Santiago y capela da Madalena. Alb.* ❻ Cima do Lugar *Priv.*
[14÷2]+ €10+€35 © 661 663 669. ❼ Arzúa *Xunta [46÷2]* (€6) © 660 396 824. ❽
Vía Láctea *Priv.[120÷10]* © 981 500 581 rua José Antonio *(adj.O Conxuro).* ❾
da Fonte *Priv.[20÷5]* © 981 501 118 Rúa do Carme 18. ❿ Los Caminantes II
Priv.[28÷1] © 647 020 600 Av. de Lugo (N-547). *Otros: (rúa Ramón Franco) P**
Casa Frade © 981 500 019. *P*' Casa Carballeira © 981 500 094 *Hs*' Mesón do
Peregrino © 981 500 830. *P*'Begoña © 981 500 517 *(BBVA). P*'Casa Nené €45+
© 981 505 107 on c/Padre Pardo,24. *N-547 H***Suiza © 981 500 862 (+1.2 km). ■
Taberna Velha: ● *(+500m) Alb.* Camiño das Ocas *Priv.[28÷5]+* €10 © 648 404
780 *N-547 Burres.* ■ Boavista: ● *(+500m) Alb.* turístico Salceda *Priv.[8÷1]+*
€12-40 © 981 502 767. ■ Salceda: N-547 *Alb.* Bondi *Priv.[30÷6]* €10 © 618 965
907. *P+Alb.*Alborada *Priv.[10÷1]+* €12 © 620 151 209 & *P***Casqueiro* © 628
558 716. ■ Brea: *CR* The Way €12-15 en suite €45 © 628 120 202 Brea 36. *O*
Empalme: El Chalet *Priv.[12÷2]+* © 659 380 723. *Alb.y rst'* Andaina *Priv.* © 981
502 925 ■ Santa Irene: ❶ *Alb.* Santa Irene *Priv.* [15÷2]* €13 © 981 511 000. ●
(+700m) ❷ *Alb.* Rural Astar *Priv.[24÷2]* €10 © 981 511 463. *Alb.* ❸ Santa Irene
Xunta.[32÷2] N-547. ■ A Rúa: *Turismo* Asoc. Hostelería Compostela © 696 652
564. *H*' O Pino © 981 511 035 N-547 *(+200m). CR* Casa Gallega © 981 511 463
opp. *CR* O Acivro €35 © 981 511 316. **Brea [0.4 km]**

■ **PEDROUZO** *Arca / O Pino:* (8 *Albergues* Av.€10): ❶ O Burgo *Priv.*[14÷1]+*
© 630 404 138 N-457 adj. Repsol. ❷ Arca *Xunta.[120÷4].* ❸ Porta de Santiago
Priv.[56÷3]* © 981 511 103. ❹ O Trisquel *Priv.[68÷5]* © 616 644 740 Rúa do
Picon. ❺ Edreira *Priv.*[48÷4]* © 981 511 365 rua Minas / c/Rua Fonte. ❻ Cruceiro
Priv.[94÷8] © 981 511 371 Av. Iglesia adj. ❼ REMhostel *Priv.[40÷1]* © 981 510
407. ❽ Otero *Priv.[36÷2]* © 671 663 374 c/ Forcarei, 2. ■ *Hostales* €15 – €45: *P*
O Muiño Mayka © 686 419 046. *Pr*' Maribel © 609 459 966 rua Mollados adj. *F*
Arca © 657 888 594. *N-547: Hs***Plantas* © 981 511 378. *P*' BuleBic © 981 511
222. *P*' Una Estrella Dorada 630 018 363. *P*' Pedrouzo © 981 510 483 *P* En Ruta
SCQ © 981 511 471 Av. de Santiago, 23. *P*'Codesal © 981 511 064 rua Codesal. *P*
Maruja © 981 511 406 rua Nova. *P*' Casal de Calma © 689 910 676 rua Igrexa.

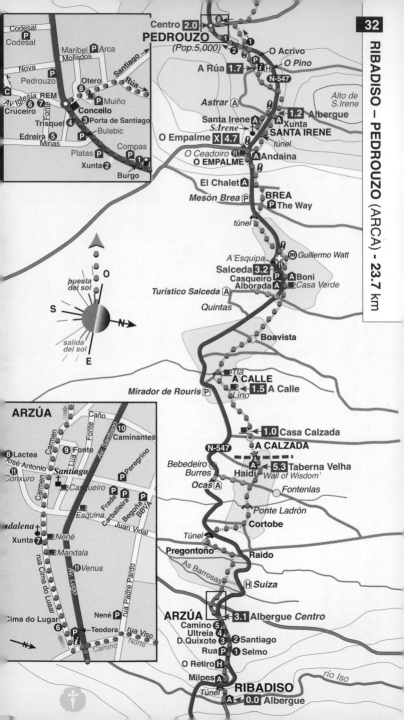

Inset map (top left):

Codesal
Codesal
Nova
Pedrouzo
Maribel P Arca
Mollados
C Cruceiro
Av. Iglesia
REM
Otero
Santiago
8
Rúa
Muiño
Concello
Trisquel 4
3 Porta de Santiago
Bulebic
Edreira 5
Minas
Platas P
Compas
Xunta 2
Burgo

Main map:

Centro **2.0**
PEDROUZO
(Pop.5,000)
O Acrivo
8
1
1
2
O Pino
A Rúa **1.7** i H
N-547
Astrar Ⓐ
Alto de
S.Irene
Santa Irene Ⓐ
S.Irene
Ⓐ Xunta **1.2** Albergue
SANTA IRENE
O Empalme ✕ **4.7**
O Ceadoiro
túnel
O EMPALME
Andaina
El Chalet Ⓐ
BREA
Mesón Brea Ⓟ
P The Way
túnel

A'Esquipa
Ⓜ *Guillermo Watt*
Salceda 3.2
Casqueiro
P
Ⓐ Boni
Alborada Ⓐ
Casa Verde
Turístico Salceda Ⓐ
Quintas

Boavista

Ⓐ **A CALLE**
Mirador de Rouris Ⓟ
1.5 A Calle
Lino

1.0 Casa Calzada
A CALZADA
N-547
Bebedeiro
Ⓐ
Burres
Haidi
5.3 Taberna Velha
Ocas Ⓐ
'Wall of Wisdom'
Fontenlas
Ponte Ladrón
Cortobe
Túnel
Pregontoño
Raido
As Barrosas
H *Suiza*

ARZÚA
3.1 Albergue *Centro*
Camino 5
Ultreia 4
2 Santiago
D.Quixote 3
Rua P 1 Selmo
O Retiro H
Milpes Ⓐ
RIBADISO
Túnel
Ⓐ **0.0** Albergue
río Iso

Compass rose:

O
puesta
del sol
S — N
salida
del sol
E

Inset map (bottom left) – ARZÚA:

Caño
Carmen
Fonte
Lúa
10
Caminantes
8 Lactea
9 Fonte
José Antonio
P Peregrino
Conxuro
Santiago
Casqueiro
P
P Frade
P
P Carballeira
Begoña
BBVA
Esquina
dalena †
Juan Vidal
Xunta 7
Nené
rua Cima do Lugar
Mandala
Av. Lugo
Ⓜ *Venus*
Nené P
rua Padre Pardo
6
P
Teodora
rua Viso
Cima do Lugar
7
Camino
Norte

33 **20.1** km (12.5 ml) – Santiago

PEDROUZO (ARCA) – SANTIAGO

▪▪▪▪▪▪▪▪	--- ---	8.0	--- ---	*40%*
▬▬▬	--- ---	7.4	--- ---	*38%*
▬▬▬	--- ---	4.4	--- ---	*22%*
Total km		**20.1** km	(12.5 ml)	

◣ --- --- 20.4 km (0.6 km)
Alto ▲ Monte do Gozo 370m (1,214 ft)
< Ⓐ Ⓗ > Amenal **3.4** km – Lavacolla **9.5** –
Monte Gozo **15.2** – S. Lázaro **17.5**

▪ **Amenal:** *H⁎⁎* **Amenal** ℂ 981 510 431. ▪ **San Paio / Aeroporto:** *Café Casa Porta de Santiago* + *P* **The Last Twelve** €40-€50 ℂ 619 904 743. *H⁎⁎⁎* **Ruta Jacobea** ℂ 981 888 211. **Lavacolla:** *P* **A Concha** €30 ℂ 981 888 390. *P⁎* **San Paio** ℂ 981 888 205. ▪ **Villamaior**: *CR* **Casa de Amancio** ℂ 981 897 086. ▪ **San Marcos** *Camping* **San Marcos**. *H⁎* **Akelarre** ℂ 981 552 689 *(+200m N-634).* ▪ **Monte del Gozo:** *Alb.* ❶ **Monte do Gozo** *Xunta.[400+]* €8. ▪ **Santiago de Compostela** *San Lazaro:* *Alb.* ❷ **Residencia de Peregrinos San Lázaro** *Xunta.[80÷6]* €10 (€7) ℂ 981 57▮ 488 adj. *Museo Pedagóxico.* *H⁎* **San Jacobo** €38 ℂ 981 580 361 Rúa de San Lázaro. 101. ▪ **San Lázaro** *opción albergues* (Av €10)*: +300m* ❸ **Fin del Camino** *Asoc. [110÷6]* €8 ℂ 981 587 324 c/Moscova / r/Roma. ❹ **Acuario** *Priv.⁎[60÷9]* ℂ 981 575 438 r/ Estocolmo 2-b. ❺ **Santo Santiago** *Priv.[40÷3]* ℂ 657 402 403 r/ Valiño 3 adj. *H* **S.Lazaro** €35+ ℂ 981 584 344. ❻ **Monterey** *Priv.[36÷3]+* ℂ 655 484 299 r/ Fontiñas 65. ❼ **La credencial** *Priv.[36÷4]* ℂ 639 966 704 r/ Fonte Concheiros 13 (r/Altiboia). ❽ **La Estrella** *Priv.[24÷1]* ℂ 881 973 926 r/ Concheiros 36 adj. ❾ **Porta Real** *Priv.[24÷9]* €10-15 ℂ 633 610 114. ❿ **Seminario Menor La Asunción** *Conv.[177]+* €10-15 ℂ 881 031 768 Av. Quiroga Palacios.

▪ **SANTIAGO DE COMPOSTELA** *Centro*: *p.108.*

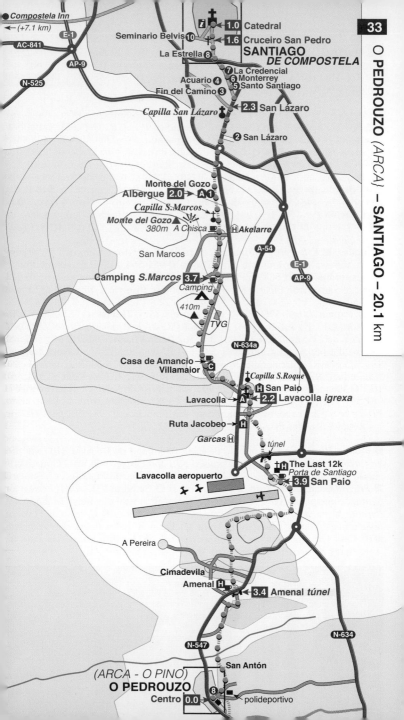

◀ Compostela Inn
(+7.1 km) ◀

E-1
AC-841
AP-9
N-525

i 1.0 Catedral
Seminario Belvis 10
1.6 Cruceiro San Pedro
La Estrella 8
SANTIAGO
DE COMPOSTELA
7 La Credencial
6 Monterrey
Acuario 4
5 Santo Santiago
Fin del Camino 3
Capilla San Lázaro 2.3 San Lázaro
2 San Lázaro

Monte del Gozo
Albergue 2.0 **A** 1
Capilla S.Marcos
Monte del Gozo ▲ *A Chisca*
380m
H *Akelarre*
San Marcos
A-54
E-1
AP-9
Camping **S.Marcos** 3.7
Camping
410m
▲
TYG
N-634a
Casa de Amancio **C**
Villamaior
†*Capilla S.Roque*
H San Paio
Lavacolla → **A** 2.2 Lavacolla *igrexa*
Ruta Jacobeo → **H**
Garcas **H**
túnel
†**H** The Last 12k
Porta de Santiago
3.9 San Paio
Lavacolla aeropuerto
✈ ✈
✈
A Pereira
Cimadevila
Amenal **H**
3.4 Amenal *túnel*
N-547
N-634
(ARCA - O PINO)
San Antón
O PEDROUZO
Centro 0.0
8
polideportivo

■ **SANTIAGO:** ❑ **Turismo:** ❖ r/Vilar, 63 ✆ 981 555 129 *June-Sept 09:00-21:00 / Oct-May 10:00-15:00 & 17:00-20:00.* **Luggage** *consigna* (Casa Ivar) ✆ 603 466 490 Trv. Universidade 1. ■ *Oficina del Peregrino* ✆ 981 568 846 – 08:00-21:00 (10:00-19:00 Nov-Mar) rua Carretas 33.

■ *Albergues:* ❶ – ⑩ (p.106) ■ *Centro €10-15:* ●11 La Salle *Priv.[84÷14]*+ ✆ 981 585 667 c/ Tras de Santa Clara. ●12 Basquiños *Priv.[10÷1]* ✆ 661 894 536 c/ Basquiños Nº45 & @ Nº67 **13 Meiga Backpackers** *Priv.[30÷5]* ✆ 981 570 846.. ■ *Centro Histórico:* ●14 O Fogar de Teodomiro *Priv.[20÷5]*+ ✆ 981 582 920 Plaza de Algalia de Arriba 3. ●15 The Last Stamp *Priv.[62÷10]* ✆ 981 563 525 rua Preguntorio 10. ●16 Azabache *Priv.[20÷5]* ✆ 981 071 254 c/Azabachería 15. ●17 Mundoalbergue *Priv.[34÷1]* ✆ 981 588 625 c/ San Clemente 26. ●18 Roots & Boots *Priv.[48÷6]* ✆ 699 631 594 rua Campo Cruceiro do Galo. ■ *Otros:* ●19 La Estación *Priv.[24÷2]* ✆ 981 594 624 rua Xoana Nogueira 14 (adj. Estación de Tren +2.9 km). ● Compostela Inn *Priv.[120÷30]*+ ✆ 981 819 030 *AC-841 (adj. Hotel Congreso +6.0 km).* ■ *Hoteles:* ■ *€30–€60:* Hs **Moure** ✆ 981 583 637 R/ dos Loureiros + *Hs* **Moure II** R/ Laureles 12. *H* **Fonte de San Roque** ✆ 981 554 447 R/ do Hospitallilo 8. **La Campana** ✆ 981 584 850 Campanas de San Juan 4. **Estrela** ✆ 981 576 924 Plaza de San Martín Pinario 5-2. *Hs* **San Martín Pinario** ✆ 981 560 282 Praza da Inmaculada. **Pico Sacro** R/ San Francisco 22 + **Pico Sacro II** ✆ 981 584 466. *Hs* **O Patron** ✆ 981 576 487 R/ das Carretas 15. *P* **Hortas** ✆ 881 259 018 R/ das Hortas 30. **La Estela** ✆ 981 582 796 R/ Raxoi 1. **Barbantes** ✆ 981 581 077 R/ do Franco 3. **Santa Cruz** ✆ 981 582 362 R/ do Vilar 42. **Suso** ✆ 981 586 611 R/ do Vilar 65. **San Jaime** ✆ 981 583 134 R/ do Vilar 12-2°. **A Nosa Casa** ✆ 981 585 926 R/ Entremuralles 9. **Mapoula** ✆ 981 580 124 R/ Entremuralles 10. **Alameda** ✆ 981 588 100 San Clemente 32. ■ *€60+:* *H* **Rua Vilar** ✆ 981 557 102 R/ Vilar 12. *H* **Airas Nunes** ✆ 902 405 858 R/ do Vilar 17. **Entrecercas** ✆ 981 571 151 R/ Entrecercas. **Costa Vella** ✆ 981 569 530 Porta de Pena 17. ■ *€100+ H****San Francisco** Campillo de San Fráncisco ✆ 981 581 634. *H****de los Reyes Católicos* Plaza Obradoiro ✆ 981582 200.

■ *Centro Histórico*: ❶ Convento de Santo Domingo de Bonaval XIII *(panteón de Castelao, Rosalía de Castro y museo do Pobo Galego).* ❷ Casa Gótica XIV *museo das Peregrinaciónes-1.* ❸ Mosteiro de San Martín Pinario XVI + *museo* ■ *Prazo Obradoiro* ❹ Pazo de Xelmirez XII ❺ Catedral XII –XVIII *Portica de Gloria, claustro, museo + tesouro da catedral* ❻ Hostal dos Reis Católicos XV *Parador* ❼ Pazo de Raxoi XVIII *Presendencia da Xunta* ❽ Colexio de Fonseca XVI *universidade y claustro.* ❾ Casa do Deán XVIII *Oficina do Peregrino.* ●10 Casa Canónica *museo Peregrinaciónes-2.* ●11 Mosteiro de San Paio de Antealtares XV *museo de Arte Sacra.* ●12 S.Maria Salomé XII.

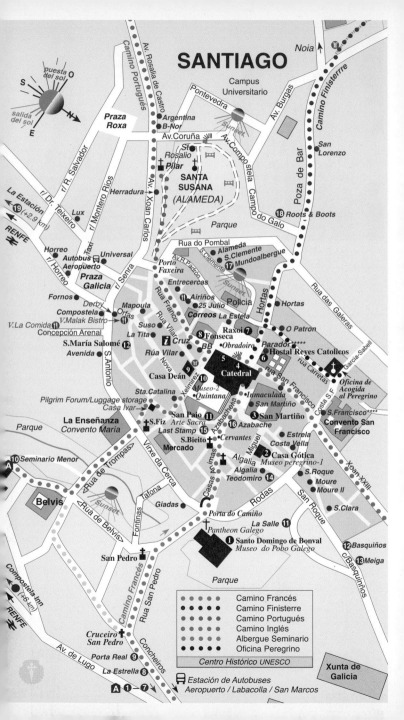

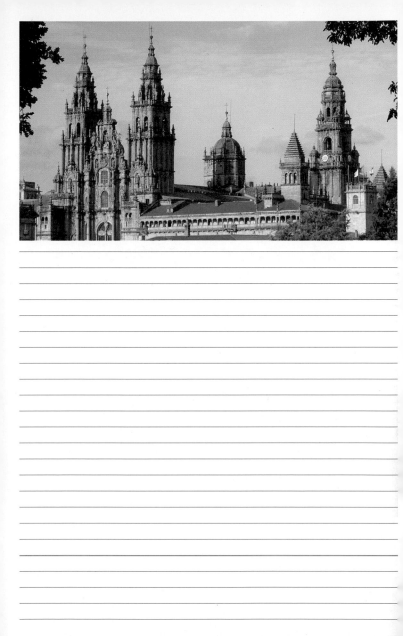

Download our Mobile Application

Available on iOS, Android and Windows Phone 8

eCamino

www.ecamino.eu

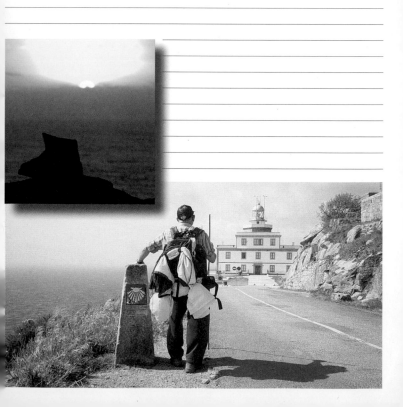

12 Caminos de Santiago

❶ Camino Francés 770 km
St. Jean / Roncesvalles – Santiago
• • • • • • • •

❷ Chemin de Paris 1000 km
Paris – St. Jean via Orléans &Tours
Alt. route from Chartres -
Soulac – Tarnos 170km
• • • • • • • •

• • • • • • • •

❸ Chemin de Vézelay 900 km
Vézelay – St. Jean via Bazas
Ext. to Namur (B) & Maastricht (NL)
• • • • • • • •

• • • • • • •

❹ Chemin du Puy 740 km
Le Puy-en-Velay – St. Jean
Ext. to Geneva, Konstanz, Prague
• • • • • • • •

❺ Chemin d'Arles 750 km
Arles – Somport Pass
Camino Aragonés 160 km
Somport Pass – Óbanos
Camí San Jaume 600 km
Port de Selva – Jaca
• • • • • • • •

• • • • • • •

❻ Camino de Madrid 320km
Madrid – Sahagún
• • • • • • • •

Camino de Levante 900 km
Valencia (Alicante) – Zamora
Alt. via Cuenca – Burgos
• • • • • • •

❼ Camino Mozárabe 390km
Granada – Mérida
(Málaga alt. via Baena)
• • • • • • •

❽ Via de la Plata 1,000km
Seville – Santiago
• • • • • • • •

❾ Camino Portugués *Central* 241km
Lisboa – Porto
Porto – Santiago
• • • • • • • •

Camino Portugués *da Costa* 372km
Porto – Caminho
Λ Guarda – Redonela
• • • • • • •

❿ Camino Finisterre 87km
Santiago – Finisterre
via – Muxía – Santiago 114 km
• • • • • • • •

⓫ Camino Inglés 110km
Ferrol – Santiago
• • • • • • •

⓬ Camino del Norte 830km
Irún – Santiago via Gijón
• • • • • • • •

Camino Primitivo 320km
Oviedo – Lugo – Melide
• • • • • • •

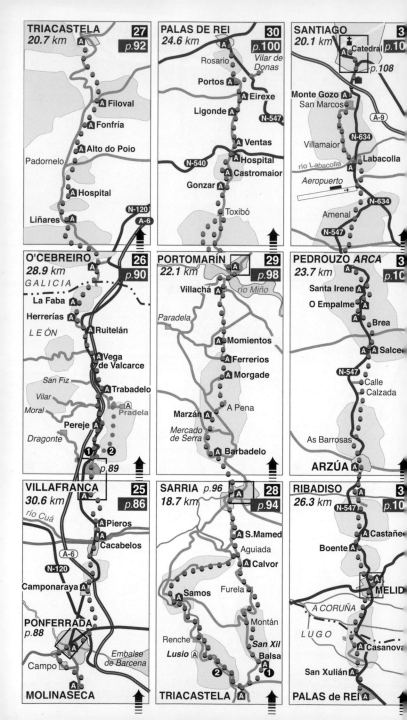

TRIACASTELA 27 — *20.7 km* — p.92

A Filoval
A Fonfría
A Alto do Poio
Padornelo
A Hospital
Liñares A
N-120 / A-6

PALAS DE REI 30 — *24.6 km* — p.100

Vilar de Donas
Rosario
Portos A
A Eirexe
Ligonde A
A Ventas
N-547
A Hospital
A Castromaior
Gonzar A
Toxibó

SANTIAGO — *20.1 km* — 3 — Catedral p.10 / p.108

Monte Gozo A
San Marcos
A-9
N-634
Villamaior
río Labacolla
Labacolla
Aeropuerto
Amenal
N-634
N-547

O'CEBREIRO 26 — *28.9 km* — p.90

GALICIA
La Faba A
Herrerías A
A Ruitelán
LEÓN
A Vega de Valcarce
San Fiz
A Trabadelo
Vilar
Moral
Pradela
Pereje
Dragonte
1 2 — p.89

PORTOMARÍN 29 — *22.1 km* — p.98

Villachá
río Miño
Paradela
A Momientos
A Ferreiros
A Morgade
A Pena
Marzán A
Mercado de Serra
A Barbadelo

PEDROUZO *ARCA* 3 — *23.7 km* — p.10

Santa Irene A
O Empalme A
A Brea
A A Salce
N-547
Calle Calzada
As Barrosas
ARZÚA A

VILLAFRANCA 25 — *30.6 km* — p.86

río Cúa
A Pieros
A Cacabelos
A-6
N-120
Camponaraya A
PONFERRADA p.88
Campo
Embalse de Barcena
MOLINASECA A

SARRIA p.96 28 — *18.7 km* — p.94

A S.Mamed
Aguiada
A Calvor
Furela
A Samos
Montán
Renche
Lusio A
San Xil
Balsa A
2 1
TRIACASTELA A

RIBADISO 3 — *26.3 km* — p.10

N-547
A Castañe
Boente A
A MELID
A CORUÑA
LUGO
A Casanova
San Xulián A
PALAS de REI A

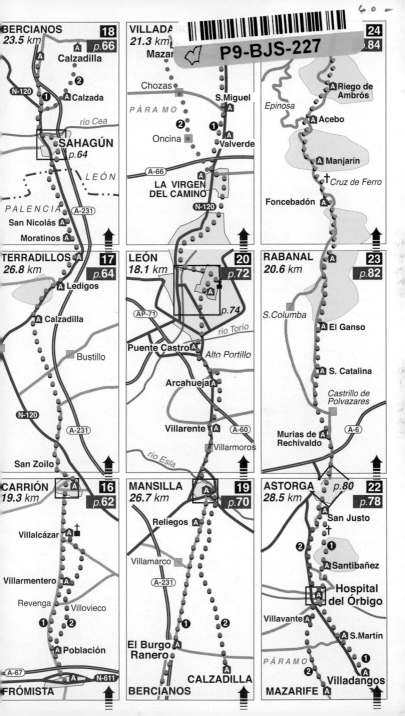

BERCIANOS 18 — *23.5 km* — p.66
Calzadilla
❷
Ⓐ Calzada — N-120 — Ⓐ ❶
río Cea
SAHAGÚN p.64
LEÓN
PALENCIA — A-231
San Nicolás Ⓐ
Moratinos Ⓐ

VILLADA 24 — *21.3 km* — p.84
Maza...
Chozas
PÁRAMO
❷ Oncina ❶ S.Miguel
A-66 Ⓐ Valverde
LA VIRGEN DEL CAMINO
N-120

Ⓐ Riego de Ambrós
Epinosa
Ⓐ Acebo
Ⓐ Manjarín
† *Cruz de Ferro*
Foncebadón Ⓐ

TERRADILLOS Ⓐ 17 — *26.8 km* — p.64
Ⓐ Ledigos
Ⓐ Calzadilla
Bustillo
N-120
A-231
San Zoilo

LEÓN 20 — *18.1 km* — p.72 / p.74
AP-71
río Torío
Puente Castro Ⓐ
Alto Portillo
Arcahueja Ⓐ
Villarente Ⓐ — A-60
Villarmoros
río Esla

RABANAL Ⓐ 23 — *20.6 km* — p.82
S.Columba
Ⓐ El Ganso
Ⓐ S. Catalina
Castrillo de Polvazares
Murias de Ⓐ Rechivaldo — A-6

CARRIÓN Ⓐ 16 — *19.3 km* — p.62
Villalcázar Ⓐ †
Villarmentero Ⓐ
Revenga ❶ Villovieco ❷
Ⓐ Población
A-67 — Ⓐ — N-611
FRÓMISTA

MANSILLA Ⓐ 19 — *26.7 km* — p.70
Reliegos Ⓐ
Villamarco
A-231
❶ ❷
El Burgo Ranero Ⓐ
BERCIANOS — **CALZADILLA** Ⓐ

ASTORGA Ⓐ 22 — p.80 — *28.5 km* — p.78
San Justo
† ❷ ❶
Ⓐ Santibañez
Ⓐ **Hospital del Órbigo**
Villavante Ⓐ
Ⓐ S.Martín
PÁRAMO ❶ ❷
Ⓐ **MAZARIFE** — Ⓐ Ⓐ Villadangos